A Boy From C-11

Case #9164

A memoir
by Harvey Ronglien

Enjoy!

*Harvey
Ronglien*

I could never forgive myself if I didn't take at least one page of this book to thank the two people who made it possible: My editor, Joan Claire Graham and my wife, Maxine Ronglien.

I thank Joan for her insight and understanding, her patience and professionalism. She is an Albert Lea writer, editor and publisher of the *Minnesota Memories* book series, and she shares my enthusiasm for preserving the history of Minnesota people and their communities. She was easy to communicate with, and working with her was a pleasure.

I have often remarked that I'm like half a pair of scissors without Maxine. I thank her for sharing my life, for understanding me, for all her sacrifices, and especially for the time, grief and joy she's experienced to hold our family together so that this book could be written. Maxine has devoted countless hours so that I could tell my story.

I will always be most grateful to these two women.

ISBN: 0971 1971 80

Chapters of My Life

A Boy From C-11

Dedicated to

the mother, whom I never knew
my wife, whom I'll forever be indebted to
and my two children,
all whose love I deeply treasure

A Boy From C-11

Forward

There were many...I was but one.

During my eleven years at the State Public School in Owatonna, Minnesota, the hills were alive with energetic children and rambunctious teenagers. Almost every day children were placed out and new ones replaced those who left. From all over the state they came--every race, color and creed. Some stayed a few days, others for many years. For some, it was a circle of hell, for others, a safe haven.

Each child has his or her own story to tell. I can only speak for myself. My memories are many of a vast, strange place that took me in from poverty's door and housed, clothed, fed and educated me. During most of my childhood years, I fully accepted the State Public School as a fulfilling home.

As an adult, I came to realize the institutional environment did not provide certain needs a child craves. Although the environment made us physically strong, it left many of us emotionally deficient. Emotional starvation is inseparable from institutional life. Due to the size of the orphanage, individual attention was minimal. Consequently, the children suffered from lack of attention, appreciation, recognition and love needed for a healthy childhood. For many it left scars that would last a lifetime.

The school did provide me with many playmates and with friendships that have lasted a lifetime. I consider all who were there my brothers and sisters. Our camaraderie is grounded in the fact that we went through childhood together.

In my opinion, the legacy of the State Public School for Dependent and Neglected Children is that the environment inherent in a large institution is not conducive to raising emotionally healthy children. Those of us who grew up there have faced lifelong challenges. May this book forever serve as a reminder of that truth and as a remembrance for every child who passed through those doors and their struggle to overcome the scars left by this institution,

Yet, it was my home, and it gave me an identity that set me apart. I'll always feel a real sense of pride in saying, "I was a State School kid!"

Harvey Ronglien--Ward of the State from 1932-1945

My Mother, Oline Bjerklie Rognlin

In the early 1990s, our adult children came home as usual to celebrate Mother's Day. That afternoon, as we sat around visiting, our 8-year-old granddaughter Tiffany stunned me with a question. "Grandpa, do you miss your mother?" Not meaning to show disrespect, I struggled with an answer.

You see, since I was separated from my mother when I was very young, I have no conscious memories of her. All I have are two pictures, taken on her wedding day. In both photographs her beautiful features look so sad. Over many years, my stock answer to any question pertaining to my mother was, "How can I miss something I never had?" That answer served as my protective shield, but today I feel remorse for hiding behind that shield.

Struggling with an answer for Tiffany that Mother's Day, I explained that all I know about my mother I learned from stories and memories my older siblings shared with me after I became an adult. They told me that our mother was a very special person, and based on the facts I was able to piece together, she certainly was remarkable.

My mother, Oline Bjerklie, was a Norwegian immigrant. In 1913, at age 19, she said goodbye to her Oslo family and sailed with other immigrants to Ellis Island. She boarded a Midwest-bound train in New York and eventually arrived in Appleton, Minnesota, where the Bakken family, her sponsors, met her and took her home.

Homesick and lonely, she found herself in a land where she could neither speak the language nor understand its culture. Work on the farm was hard, and whatever her dreams for happiness might have been, they were never fulfilled. In fact, her dreams were shattered time and time again.

By her twenty-fourth birthday, Oline had blossomed into a beautiful young lady. Many referred to her as the beauty of Swift County. It's no wonder a high-spirited, fun-loving neighbor fellow by the name of Eddie took a special interest in her. They shared time at basket socials, buggy riding, and barn dancing. Probably Eddie's main attraction was that he made her feel wanted by showing her love and attention that she had missed as a girl. Her mother had died when she was 11 years old, and her father remarried twice. She told my older siblings that her second stepmother was a cruel woman.

Before long, Oline was pregnant, and she and Eddie were married on August 24, 1917. It wasn't exactly a union made in heaven. Instead, it was a union that produced tragedy and heartache beyond belief. She soon came to realize that her Lancelot was a hard-drinking, irresponsible, and immutably immature mate, and their marriage produced nine children in twelve years.

A devoted Christian, Mother's social life revolved around Long Lake Lutheran Church. Dad's social life revolved around the saloons. While eking out an existence on a small Minnesota farm with poor soil during the 1920s, Mother never had a day of rest. The cows had to be milked, the livestock had to be fed, and the barn needed to be cleaned.

Mother often milked cows alone while my father played with the kids or stayed too long in town. Harvest time often found her pleading with neighbors to help her and the older children bring in the crops while Eddie was off on still another drinking spree. She had to sew, wash clothes, cook, bake and can food for her large family. Winter cold brought on the added chore of gathering and chopping wood to burn in the old kitchen range and potbellied stove. Of course, there was no running water or electricity.

One evening while she was out milking cows, the young children in the house began playing with matches, and a curtain caught fire. Everyone survived, but our home and meager possessions were lost. Then, baby Hallen died from an acute ear infection. The Great Depression added to her woes.

Her hard life, coupled with nine successive pregnancies and nursing babies, soon took its toll on her small body. Now wracked with tuberculosis of the throat, she was constantly coughing and spitting up blood. My oldest sister Hazel remembers a crimson trail of blood on the snow between the house and barn.

Despite her failing health, Mother adamantly refused to leave her family. Eventually, however, the doctor persuaded her to go to the State TB Sanatorium at Walker, Minnesota, promising her that she would only be gone for six months.

Before leaving, she made arrangements with the Bakken family to take care of baby Gladyce. As she prepared to leave, she baked bread and cookies and made sure all the laundry was done. On her last night at home, she prepared a duck supper for her family. In the kitchen, she begged my sister Hazel to keep the family together, because she would soon be home.

Early the next morning, Mother and Pa left for Walker. Soon after that, Grandma Rognlin and others came in and threw away all the bread and food our mother had prepared for fear we children would catch tuberculosis from eating them. They also scrubbed the house and burned all our straw mattresses. Finally they left Hazel, age 12, in charge.

Hazel now became "Mother." She was frequently forced to miss school in order to care for us. Grandma Rognlin would come over occasionally, but she was crabby and she would hide any baked goods. We kids only wanted Hazel. Hazel baked bread, cookies or cakes in the old kitchen range. Sometimes they turned out, and other times they didn't, but we were hungry and we ate it.

With my little sister gone, I once again became the baby of the family. I was 4 years old, but Hazel would rock me to sleep every night. It was the only way I would settle down for the night.

My sister Ruth recalls that in the evenings we would all go out and climb on top of the threshing machine, face north, wave and ask, "When are you coming home, Moder?" We spoke Norwegian, our mother's native tongue, and while she was gone we counted the days till her return.

Meanwhile, at the sanatorium, six months passed, and our mother's health had not improved. Mother pleaded with the sanatorium staff to allow her to return home just once to see her children. They finally agreed, and Pa went to get her. But when she arrived home she found that in her absence, well-meaning relatives had warned her children that they should not go near her for fear they would contract tuberculosis from her.

My mother, her body now ravaged and her voice nearly silenced by the illness that would soon consume her, could barely get out a raspy whisper as she reached out to embrace her beloved children. Believing what they had been told about contracting her illness, her frightened children cowered and rejected her open arms. This was the last time we saw our beloved mother.

With her world totally shattered, she returned to the sanatorium, surrendered her will to live, and eventually succumbed. My mother died in 1934 at the age of 39.

My answer today to my granddaughter's question is this: Yes, I miss my mother. I just wish I could have known her--to see how she walked across the room, how she smiled, how she sat in a chair. I wish I remembered her hands or her pretty, wavy hair.

Most of all I wish I could have said, "Mom, I love you."

A Boy From C-11

My Father, Eddie Rognlin, and His Legacy

Eddie Rognlin was born in 1893 and raised on a farm near Appleton, Minnesota. He had two sisters and a brother, but his father was out of the picture relatively soon, either because of alcoholism or mental illness--we're not sure. Their mother Annie basically raised Eddie and his siblings. Although his siblings grew to be somewhat responsible adults, Eddie entered adulthood with character flaws. He was not a mean man, but he was a follower and an alcoholic. Uneducated and illiterate, he lacked the ability to set goals or handle responsibility.

When he worked, he worked hard as a farm hand, but he was not dependable. Whenever he had the urge to drink, he would go on a binge, often ending up in jail.

It's easy to understand that without my mother to pick up the pieces and give him some routine or structure, Eddie lost all control of his life after she went to the sanatorium. Not long after he was left with eight children in November of 1931, he went out with some friends for a Saturday night of drinking. On the way home they came up with the crazy idea to break into a country school.

They stole some things and vandalized the building. Eddie volunteered his barn to store the loot so they dropped it all off at our farm. The next morning, when reality hit, Eddie took a shovel and started to bury the stolen books, maps and classroom supplies.

When word of this misdeed got out in the community, the likely suspects included my father. He became worried and prepared his children. "If the sheriff comes, don't tell him where Pa is."

Sure enough, the sheriff did come calling when my older sisters and brothers were at school, and my brother Oscar and I were home with Pa. Oscar was 5 years old, and I was 4. When Pa saw a car coming up our long driveway, he bolted out the back door to hide outside. Both Oscar and I remember the knock on the door; in fact, it is my one and only memory of home. We boys wore very little clothing. The sheriff ruffled our hair and asked us where Pa was. When we refused to speak, the sheriff offered us candy. Feeling more comfortable, we both responded to the sheriff's question, but we lied as Pa had told us to do. I guess that teaching us to lie was part of Pa's legacy to us boys.

Details are vague as to what happened next, but the sheriff or his men found Pa on the farmyard along with some evidence. Oscar and I watched as they handcuffed Pa and hauled him away. When we saw our older brothers and sisters walking up the driveway from school, we ran to them crying, "They put iron on Pa's wrists and took him away." That whole sequence of events makes up my only childhood memory of my father.

After watching the sheriff lead him away in handcuffs, I did not see my Pa again for many years. We children were not aware that his trial took place just a few days after his arrest. An article in the *Appleton Press,* dated November 20, 1931, states that Eddie Rognlin who was 38 years old, had been sentenced by the judge the previous Thursday to serve sentence of no more than two years at Stillwater State Prison for breaking into the schoolhouse and taking away much of the schoolroom equipment. His two accomplices received similar sentences for the crime of burglary.

With both parents now out of the picture, we eight children were now totally abandoned. County commissioners and the Probate Court were forced to find homes for us. My baby sister Gladyce had already settled in with the Bakken family, an arrangement made with my mother's blessing. Hazel, then 13, struggled with my mother's plea to keep the family together, with a youngster's optimistic belief that her mother would soon be coming home. But how could Hazel continue to care for a family at such a tender age?

County commissioners and other authorities, who were responsible for the welfare of dependent and neglected children in those days, understood the scope of the problem and reacted pragmatically to this terrible situation, and their judgment prevailed. They initiated the legal procedure that would declare us all Wards of the State.

Times were hard. Minnesota, like the rest of the nation, was struggling through the depths of the Great Depression. Bread lines were common, and unemployment nationally soared to 25%. In rural Minnesota, unemployment may have been even higher than the national figure, and loss of jobs was taking a heavy toll on families. In Appleton and Benson, farmers were struggling to hang on to their farms. Barely able to make ends meet with their own families, who among them would be able to take in an extra child? A child too young to help with farm or housework would have been more burdensome than an older child with some skills.

Word was passed around in the community. Who would be able to take in one of the Rognlin children? On a cool November day after Pa was tried and sentenced by the district court in Benson, seven of us were taken to that same Swift County Courthouse.

My sister believes that we were all supposed to go to the State Public School for Dependent and Neglected Children in Owatonna. The problem with this plan was that the State School was operating beyond full capacity with 522 children, and the school was experiencing hard times. In 1931, with the unfortunate combination of fewer families able to adopt a child and an increased need for placement of dependent children, the State School system was experiencing a crunch.

An article in the *Owatonna People's Press* reported on March 5, 1932, that 193 children's names were on the waiting list to get in. The headline read, "Enrollment at State School is Precarious. Hard Times Increase Commitments, Decrease Adoptions."

Those who were in charge of us children opted to try to find a quick solution to our problem within our own community. First we were lined up on the steps of the courthouse, and someone took one last picture of all of us together. Then someone made a plea for community members to take one of us and give us a home.

Hazel remembers that there was a lot of confusion. People whispered, conferred, and moved from room to room. The authorities were doing their best to deal with this human tragedy.

One by one, locals stepped up to claim a child and give him or her a home. At the end of the process, Oscar and I stood alone. No one wanted rambunctious 4 and 5-year-old boys who couldn't earn their keep. Until we got bigger and stronger, we would only be nuisances or additional mouths to feed. As we watched our older brothers and sisters leave to go home with other people, we must have felt totally abandoned.

Since nobody wanted us, authorities still had to deal with the problem of figuring out what to do with Oscar and me, the two littlest guys. Their only solution was for the County Commissioners to take us home temporarily, so we separated to go with different commissioners. Now separated from our older siblings, our parents, and each other, Oscar and I were truly alone. To compound our fear and isolation, we spoke only Norwegian in these English-speaking homes.

My sister Hazel recalls that I was placed in three different homes over the next year. No doubt, I stayed in each place just long enough to find a comfort zone before I was uprooted to move on to the next place. Since Oscar and I were so little, we did not know that our names were working their way up the waiting list at the State Public School for Dependent and Neglected Children in Owatonna. Our numbers finally came up on November 1, 1932.

Pa's two years in Stillwater State Prison and the dissolution of his family was a huge price to pay for one night of drinking and carousing. But after we had all grown up and he had resumed life as a free man, we reunited with him and saw that his alcoholism continued for two decades. This problem drove him, led him to engage in more irresponsible behavior, and caused his death in 1956 at age 63. He died of a broken neck after he opened the wrong door and fell down some basement stairs. We children took up a collection to bury him.

Eddie Rognlin

My parents, Oline Bjerklie and Eddie Rognlin, tied the knot on August 24, 1917. It's a good thing that they had this picture taken, because I have no conscious memory of her.

My big brothers Leonard and Ruben, and my older sisters Verna, Ruth, and Hazel posed with Oscar and me on the courthouse steps. It would be twenty-five years before we all stood together again. Before going to the State School, I stayed with some people who found me a nice coat and hat and took these photos.

State School Bound

On November 1, 1932, nearly one year after my father was sentenced to two years at Stillwater State Prison, Sheriff Ed Flaten loaded Oscar and me into his Model A Ford. We were destined to go on a 250-mile trip that would forever change our lives. I remember being given a candy bar en route. Our unknown destination was paved by circumstances beyond our control, and the rearview mirror framed a picture of our shattered family as we pulled away from Swift County.

After hours of anticipation, fear and apprehension, the two smallest occupants of this little car, under the cover of darkness, rolled onto the grounds of the State Public School for Dependent and Neglected Children in Owatonna, Minnesota.

Four months earlier, crowded conditions had been eased somewhat by the opening of two new cottages, each with enough room to house thirty boys. As we stopped in front of a big brick building that we would get to know as Cottage-12, I stepped out passively and started walking toward the entrance. Pretty soon I heard Oscar screaming, kicking and yelling, "I want to go home!" Someone forced him out of the car and took him into C-12 to join me.

My only memories of that first night at C-12 are of watching Oscar being pulled from that car and receiving a bowl of soup when I got inside. We learned later that every child had to spend his or her first three weeks in C-12, quarantined in case we carried disease or parasites. We were fed, cleaned, deloused, clothed, evaluated and immunized there.

Oscar and I were now "State School Kids." I'm sure it was human error, but they changed our last name from Rognlin to Ronglien. We didn't realize this for many years. When we were old enough to read the letters my sister Hazel sent us, we saw our names on the envelopes and thought it was strange that she didn't know how to spell our last name. Someone also changed my birth date, an error I didn't learn about until I obtained a birth certificate prior to entering the Army.

After three weeks in the detention cottage, I was transferred to C-6, the small boys' cottage. Oscar went to C-11, a new cottage for boys age 6 to 14. We were separated socially and could only see each other in passing on the sidewalk or in the dining room.

Case #9164

I was now case #9164 in a state institution. Our case numbers were determined by the order in which we arrived, so since the State School for Dependent and Neglected Children had been in existence since 1886, my case number was fairly high. I became one of 500 children housed on the grounds in 1932, and we had come from all parts of Minnesota. By the time the school closed in 1945, 10,635 case numbers had been assigned.

Galen Merrill was school superintendent, a position he had held since the school opened, and very few policies or procedures had changed in the 46 years he had been in charge. Mr. Merrill was a hands-on administrator, which meant that occasionally he would personally enforce rules.

When we children entered the State School, we became Wards of the State, and all parental rights were permanently revoked. Our ages ranged from newborns to 18. Once admitted to the Minnesota State School for Dependent and Neglected Children, we became part of an institutional system based on four cornerstones: 1. Family-like life in cottages 2. Placing-out program 3. Emphasis on discipline and useful labor 4. Education.

Initially, when the place was established in the Victorian era, the over-all mission of the school was to provide an interim home before placing children for adoption. However, adoption rates were extremely low (5%) so many older children were placed out on indenture contracts until age 18.

Some children found good homes through the indenture arrangement, but others were not so fortunate. Siblings may have entered the school together, but later some were separated with no explanation about where the placed-out sibling went. Some never found each other again. Over the years the size of the institution grew, more buildings were built, and the original 160-acre campus more than doubled. The *St. Paul Pioneer Press* reported in 1922 that the State School was the third largest orphanage in the nation, and the largest west of the Mississippi.

Wherever we children came from, it had to have been chaotic, or why would we have been sent to this place? For the first time in many of our lives we experienced security, stability and structure. We had three meals a day, a clean environment, a warm bed, clothes and shoes, good education, good medical and dental care and good moral and religious training. We also had plenty of playmates.

While the intent of the school's founders was not to institutionalize children, those who stayed for any length of time indeed became institutionalized. The sheer size of the place, combined with strict adherence to routine, lack of parental type affection from caregivers, and lack of influence from the outside world created a complete institutional environment, and the children who lived there were affected.

Unfortunately, anyone who lived in this environment for many years, like I did, would most likely become emotionally and socially crippled due to lack of love, appreciation, and a family environment that a normal home provides. This has affected us throughout our lives.

The State School for Dependent and Neglected children was more like a village than a school so there was very little reason for any of us to ever venture beyond our campus. The school was self-sufficient. Children lived in sixteen cottages, where a live-in matron and her assistants cared for 25-35 youngsters. Other buildings included a nursery, hospital, school, gymnasium, laundry, and superintendent and employee residences.

The school had its own water tower and power plant, and an underground tunnel connected every major building. Electrical power lines and steam heat pipes ran through these tunnels that were big enough to walk through, and I can't remember that we were ever without electricity or heat, despite storms and winds that from time to time darkened the rest of the town of Owatonna.

A large root cellar stored fruits and vegetables grown on our farm and garden, and we drank milk from our own cows, ate meat from our own swine and beef, and eggs from our own chickens. We had a granary, and our bakery produced enough bread to feed more than 500 children and staff. Our icehouse stored ice year-round to assure additional cold storage of dairy, meat and produce back in the days when refrigerators were small, and our greenhouse helped provide some kids with horticulture training. We had a carpentry shop, a gym with a basketball court, a running track, and an indoor swimming pool, and we all learned to swim.

A cinder path led the way to the children's cemetery. More than 300 children died while under state guardianship, and 198, unclaimed by family, are buried in the cemetery. Eleven children died during my eleven years at the school. During the early years, tombstones were erected. When the state discontinued funding this practice, children were buried with their case numbers etched on little cement slabs.

The Main Building served as the school's nerve center. Its middle section housed the administration staff and a visiting room. The left wing contained the small boys' living area, and the right wing housed the first chapel/auditorium. The dining rooms were located in the back. The lower level contained a kitchen, bakery, barbershop, shoe repair, butcher shop, milk pasteurizer, supplies and storage. The upper floors provided employees' living quarters, sewing room and linen storage. Sidewalks connected various buildings on the campus, and also served as boundaries for each cottage's play area.

The school's policy stated, "Order, usefulness and discipline will be stressed, as well as obedience and efficiency. Gentle and loving measures will be advocated, but the value of drill, discipline and labor can never be underestimated. It is believed labor, no matter how dreary the task or how paltry the remuneration, is good for children. Each child, no matter the age, should be part of some worthwhile, demanding activity each day."

This place with its unchanging routine became my life for eleven years. With little reason or opportunity to go off these grounds, this is where my world existed, day after day, year after year, with little change of pace.

C-11

After a year of a somewhat softer life in the small boys' cottage, I was transferred to Cottage 11 for boys age 6-14. Although I was at the bottom of the pecking order age-wise and experience-wise, I was so happy to be reunited in C-11 with my brother Oscar. Miss Morgan was my new matron, and under her rule I quickly learned about regimentation and discipline. I also quickly fell into the negative effects of institutional environment.

Our social order was very importantly governed by unwritten rules, similar to those observed by prison inmates:

1. The strong ruled.
2. Snitching, on peers or employees, was a cardinal sin.
3. It was you against authority.
4. Every cottage had a pecking order.

After awhile each child knew how much he had to take or not take from the other kids, and he came to understand his place in the pecking order. Certain things didn't seem right, but I learned to follow institutional tradition. Each new kid fell into line, and he would be on the giving end when the next new kid arrived. It's just the way it was.

Every day in Cottage 11 presented a competitive obstacle course, starting at 6 a.m. We had two bathrooms, and each contained two urinals, two toilets and four washbasins, and all 35 of us needed to use them NOW. To further complicate the situation, each kid was aggressive, determined and tough.

We were dressed basically alike in light colored shirts, knickers, high brown socks and "clodhopper" high-top leather shoes made by the Red Wing Shoe Company. No one had his own clothing. The matron simply dealt out clothing after our Saturday night bath. We received an outfit for church and school and another outfit for work and play. Everything was neat and orderly because Miss Morgan wanted our appearance to reflect well on her.

After we washed and dressed, we went to sit in our chair in the basement. When everyone had gathered, we walked two by two over to the dining room for breakfast, which every day was the same--mush. I suppose it was oatmeal or cornmeal, but we called it mush, and we ate it because there would be no more food until lunch.

When we returned to our cottages, each of us had an assigned job. We scrubbed floors, made beds, dusted or cleaned bathrooms. When that was done, we left for school, again walking by twos, the shortest to the tallest. We walked like that whenever we went out as a cottage, whether to meals, school or church.

After school it was playtime, and each game was a competitive feud. The hard surface playground was like a combat zone, with enjoyment on winning. Those who lacked competitive drive and athletic prowess had very little fun. During warm weather, the assistant matron sat out on the front step knitting or darning, keeping a watchful eye as we played outside. During bad weather we played in the basement. We paid no attention to thermometer readings. When it was cold we put on a jacket, and when it warmed up we took it off.

The end of each day was another exercise in guile, speed and strength as we jockeyed for a place in the front of the line to wash up, brush teeth and use the urinal. Bedtime was 7:30 year round, with no exceptions. We ended each day kneeling by the side of our beds saying the Lord's Prayer. We were not allowed to talk after lights out.

Ralph, the night watchman, would come through twice each night to wake the bed wetters. Ralph had club feet that faced in toward each other, and he had to step one foot over the other. I can still hear his clump, clump, clump coming up the marbled stairs. Unfortunately, his efforts didn't always prevent accidents. I don't know about the girls, but there was a lot of bed wetting in the boys' cottages. Recently I heard a professional explain that bed wetting is common in children who experience severe trauma in their early years.

At mealtime, we always sat in the same chair in the dining room, at tables that held ten people, and the ritual was the same at every meal. When we were all seated, Miss McGregor, head of dining services, hit a bell, and we would bow our heads and say grace silently. After about a minute she hit the bell again to end the prayer. Don't ask me how many actually prayed.

Each table handled its food differently. Some assigned to the head of the table a kid who filled plates and passed them to the others. Others passed bowls around so diners could help themselves. The food wasn't Mom's cooking, but it was nutritious, and we always had enough food to eat and three meals a day. There was always plenty of milk and bread and lots of cooked vegetables. To this day I cannot stand the odor of cooked vegetables, and I refuse to eat them.

We also had lots of stew and ginger snap cookies. We learned to eat what they served us because there was absolutely no snacking between meals. In winter they gave us cod liver oil pills before the evening meal to replace sunshine, but many pills ended up under the table.

To signal the end of each meal, a final bell rang, and we filed back to our cottages to get ready for whatever our next activity was--school, church, play time or chores. After every meal a group of kids, both boys and girls, had the responsibility to scrub all the dining room floors on their hands and knees. The floors were covered with ceramic tile, and if a dirty or wet shoe ever tracked in mud or dirt, the floors remained dirty only for the time it took for the diners to consume their meal. A few minutes after the closing bell, all those tiles became spotlessly clean again. A common memory of State Schoolers is the everlasting scrubbing, waxing and polishing of floors, not only in the dining room, but also in cottages.

The image of the school and of each cottage was all-important, far more important than our individual comfort, and we had to pitch in to maintain a pristine, well-ordered image in case someone from outside should ever stop in to take a peek. We weren't allowed to use our pillows for sleeping. Before bedtime we had to neatly remove our pillows and lay them on the floor, and in the morning we had to properly make our beds with our pillows displayed against our headboards, without a wrinkle. We had to clean the living room every day, yet we were not allowed to use that room or that comfortable furniture unless a visitor arrived, and that didn't happen very often. If we weren't sleeping or cleaning, the only inside area we were allowed to use was the basement.

This is an early picture of the campus of the State School, as viewed from the east. In the foreground is the nursery, and in the distance are cottages, the Main Building, water tower, fields, and smoke stacks, evidence of the self-sufficiency of the place.

C- 11, built in the '20s, is referred to as "The New Cottage," on a postcard that was probably sold to Owatonna residents and visitors. The word "cottage" suggests hominess, even though this large building does not fit the usual definition of a cottage.

These are C-11 boys, dressed for school in the top photo. I am the one nodding off in the second row. In the lower picture, we are dressed for play. Oscar is on the left; I am in the center.

Another postcard, this one shows the formidable Main Building. From the looks of the cars, this must have been taken during the time I was there.

This photo of the old school building, with children and adults posing on the lawn, shows an idyllic view of a place where 500 children and many adults lived, worked and learned.

Diners bowed their heads and said a silent prayer.

Even toddlers enjoyed the Fourth of July picnic.

Our playground equipment accommodated vigorous physical activity.

Grade School

Education was another cornerstone of the State School. "The State Public School will be a state primary school where the children, until they can be adopted or indentured, can be educated morally and mentally, and also taught habits of industry. This training will be of great practical value to them and to their foster parents, as hundreds of children go out from the school into the homes of our citizens every year."

I have an early memory of sitting on the curb watching the new school being built in 1933. I was living in the small boys' cottage, and I went on to attend that new school from first through eighth grade. We had self-contained classrooms, and one teacher taught all subjects.

Our new school contained an auditorium where we put on plays and had lyceums, which were educational programs. At Christmas time and each spring, we put on an operetta and invited the community to attend. We also used the auditorium for Sunday church services, funerals, and Wednesday night movies. All children on the campus attended these functions.

We left the school building and walked over to the gymnasium for gym classes. We had a large indoor swimming pool and a wading pool for the little children. Everyone learned to swim. Tumbling was big, and our tumblers performed at places like the State Fair, but I preferred basketball and baseball.

As a young child, I thought all teachers were very nice, but I can't remember receiving extra attention from them.

Although teachers seemed to better understand a child's needs, no one ever took the time to explain why education was important to our future. I simply went to school. Maybe that accounts, in part, for my lack of interest in school, but then, I wasn't the brightest bulb on the tree. One drawback of our system was that if you failed one subject you would have to take the entire grade over again. Therefore, many State School kids were older than their high school classmates. Arithmetic was my downfall, and I failed fifth and seventh grades.

I don't remember that school was ever closed for a snowstorm or for any other reason. I don't remember that we ever had homework or attended summer school. In addition to our regular subjects, girls learned home economics and boys took shop. I wasn't very good in shop class either.

Those who remained at the State School beyond their grammar school years went to Owatonna High School, and for most it was their first real exposure to regular life in the outside world. Girls rode a bus to high school, and boys were trucked in the back of a cattle truck. As for being taught "habits of industry," we each had daily jobs that we were responsible for before and after school. Without question, the goal was to keep us busy, and that wasn't bad. We learned how to work.

Good Times and Bad Times

People who hear about the discipline we endured might make the mistake of thinking we had no fun, or no social life, but such was not the case. Recreation and play were an integral part of our schedule. During winter, areas were flooded for skating, and we loved sledding and playing in the snow. The presence of many playmates kept us engaged in vigorous outdoor play year-round. Like kids everywhere, we gave each other nicknames like Pickerseat, Lincoln, Bookworm, Moose, Squarehead and mine--Skippy. We had very little knowledge of Owatonna kids our age, and we dismissed them with the label "downtown kids." During warmer weather we took advantage of the recreational opportunities provided by the school as we climbed on monkey bars, rode on swings and seesaws, swam in the pool, and played ball, leapfrog, tag and marbles.

As summer neared, we "readied our skin for the summer sun" by lying on the sidewalk, fifteen minutes on our backs and then fifteen minutes on our stomachs. Summertime, with no school, was the greatest fun. Except for a few hours on Sunday, we never wore a pair of shoes. It was a thrill when Miss Morgan said we could go and play softball on "the greens," the big grassy area behind the school. Softball games between cottages were very competitive. We loved to play marbles for keeps, and since we had no money, marbles became our trading currency, and the guy with the most marbles was held in high esteem. We also enjoyed playing jacks, running, jumping and fighting. Occasionally we would slink down to the apple orchard and watermelon patch. Oh, how we liked to outwit authority!

Not everything about summer was fun. Our housecleaning jobs were extensive and included washing all the windows and taking all our mattresses outside for their annual beatings. We stepped up our efforts to clean and wax the floor of the living room, which we were not allowed to use. I hated all these jobs.

One time they assigned me the job of being a waiter for the matrons. I was serving rhubarb sauce with a sauce dish in each hand. As I reached over with one hand to put the first dish down, I poured a dish full of sauce on the head of the matron who was sitting nearest my other hand. That ended my career as a waiter.

During the school year, we had our own activities and high school athletic teams. We'd play Faribault School for the Deaf, Hayfield, Ellendale and some of the B-squad teams in southern Minnesota's Big-9 Conference. We did well, considering that our top athletes were playing for Owatonna High School. We had Boy Scouts too, and some earned Eagle badges, but I never participated.

Not only did we play sports, but also we were sports fans. I remember listening to Golden Gopher football games on the radio, and I still remember names like Buhler, Beise, Widseth, Uram, Gimitro and Wildung. I remember listening to Joe Louis fights. We also listened to baseball games. Joe Louis and Lou Gehrig, my childhood heroes, were bigger than life. Radio brought us other types of heroes too. I remember the news when Amelia Earhart's plane went down somewhere in the South Pacific the summer of 1937.

Radio did not provide our only link to entertainment and the outside world. A recreational highlight of our week was "Wednesday night at the movies," held right after supper. Westerns were our favorites, and I'm sure we saw every one ever made. Every once in awhile some wise guy would start a rumor that the next movie would be a love story, and all the boys would groan and moan and act relieved when the usual Western showed up on the screen. Having to miss the movie was a common punishment, and that really hurt.

Various celebrations scattered throughout the calendar provided a welcome break from routine, and the Fourth of July always made the summer memorable and special. It was the only time when boys and girls could play together in foot races, sack races, a peanut scramble and a tug of war. At 4 p.m. we'd each get a chocolate-covered ice cream bar on a stick--called a Cheerio, and the day ended with a movie in the auditorium. Other great summer days included an annual picnic day at Mineral Springs Park, an afternoon at the Steele County Fair, and a 13-mile bus trip to Clear Lake in Waseca for an afternoon at the beach. Those were real treats. October 11, Armistice Day, was called "Cracker Jack Day." We each received a box of Cracker Jacks, a big treat. We were told it was a token payment to kids who had lost their fathers in wars. Thanksgiving dinner was a cut above average, with turkey, mashed potatoes, and cranberries.

Christmas was also special. Each cottage had a tree, and it was the only time we were allowed to go into the living room and the only time we were allowed to stay up until 9 p.m. We each received about three small gifts that might include jacks, marbles, tops, harmonicas, Rose's Hair Oil, lotion and yo-yos.

In addition, the Rotarians came to our auditorium every Monday before Christmas and sang carols with us, led by Harry Wenger, Owatonna High School choir director. They gave us each a small box filled with hard candy, an apple and an orange.

Valentines Day was memorable too. Each grade had its own Valentine box, and we made our Valentines from colored construction paper and paste. It was very important to see who got the most Valentines and what was written on them. I was pretty well liked by my classmates so I was never disappointed.

Since most aspects of our lives were so strictly regulated, our recreation time provided a very important social and energy outlet. One summer day when I was a young teenager, I got caught stealing a magazine from Steve's Cigar Store while others attended a movie in the downtown theater. My records show that the police were called; they took me to the police station, and called someone at the school, who came and got me. My punishment was having to do extra chores in the cottage and then stand in the cottage entrance during recreation time for two months, where I could see but not join the others having a good time outside. That was torture.

Authority figures often confuse punishment with discipline. The word "discipline" means to teach, and while it is possible to teach someone a lesson by punishing him, it is not usually the most effective approach. Dwain Duis, an older State School boy who was going to Owatonna High School, taught me a lesson that proved far more effective. He told me that when I stole that magazine, I made all the State School kids look bad. He explained that we already had two strikes against us to start

42

with, and he explained that it looked bad to townspeople when I shoplifted, and their negative opinion affected not just me, but all State Schoolers. I never forgot that lesson.

Dwain was quite a remarkable young man. He was very popular at Owatonna High School, where he became a class officer and had the lead role in the senior class play. This was highly unusual for a State School kid. The State School authorities also let him have a part-time job downtown. Although he was held in high regard outside the school, his life at the school was very hard. He wasn't a jock, and he didn't fit in with the guys. A popular name for kids like Dwain was "sissy." Those who got good grades were called "bookworm."

With his part-time job earnings, Dwain purchased a small bottle of perfume for his high school girlfriend. Someone from the store wrapped and ribboned it for him, but he couldn't give it to her until the next day so he hid it in the cottage. Somehow some wise guy got wind of it and told the others, and they scavenged and searched until they found it. Then they unwrapped it, poured out the perfume, urinated in it and put it all back together again. One kid had the courage to tell the matron, and she had to call Dwain in and tell him what had happened. It broke his heart. I'm sure what made this even more devastating was the fact that Dwain had to take it. He wasn't the type who could even the score with scoundrels. Not all of our social interaction was good hearted. Like all kids, we could be cruel, and Dwain got picked on because he refused to fight back.

Occasionally older kids were allowed to work downtown. I remember kids caddying at the Owatonna Country Club, making 50 cents or 75 cents a day. Kids worked at the Owatonna

Canning Company and Cashman's Nursery. I worked at the nursery pulling little trees out of the wet mud. It was cold and hard work. We would get paid in cash, and then we'd have to turn the money in to the school office for safekeeping.

Like boys everywhere, sometimes we talked about going to faraway places and having fantasy adventures. The lure of railroad tracks that passed nearby was more than some kids could resist, no matter the penalty. We fantasized that two notorious gangsters of the '30s, John Dillinger and Machine Gun Kelly, were hiding near the tracks west of our school. Oh, to be a bum riding the rails to unknown, exciting destinations. We commonly waved at hobos who were riding the freights and threw them green apples. One day a hobo came up on the grounds and talked a boy into exchanging his worn-out shoes for the boy's good pair. Darned if he didn't pull off the trade. The boy later paid dearly for this transaction when the matron noticed and said, "Where did you get THOSE shoes?" I don't remember his specific punishment, but I'm sure the boy never forgot it.

Religion was part of our lives, and every Sunday morning at 9 we attended church services in the auditorium. Each week a different pastor or priest conducted a service at our level, and we all got saved before going back to our sinning ways on the playground. When we were old enough for confirmation, we were allowed to walk to catechism class at our preferred church downtown on Saturday mornings. I can remember stealing money from glass milk bottles left on porches. I guess my religious training had a few holes in it. One part of religion that has stuck with me all these years is the hymns we would sing. I still love them.

In 1934 Galen Merrill, the Coldwater, Michigan professor who had been the superintendent of the State School since it opened in 1886, died. The institution had grown tremendously, but had otherwise gone on with very few changes under his leadership for nearly a half century. Children and staff attended his funeral on the campus, and then a second funeral was held at his downtown church. Many of the older kids were crying, but I wasn't crying, and I wondered why. I was only 7 years old, and although I knew he was a respected figure, I had never talked to him. I was too young to understand death.

As I became older, death became more of a reality when some of the children I knew suddenly died. There was never any counseling or discussion of death with our matron, teachers or anyone else that I can remember. I recall funerals for Vernon Hadley, who drowned, and Guy Chatfield, who died after a long illness. I remember the agony of David Freeman, who broke his neck during a sandlot football game. He died the next day. Another boy was killed while retrieving a ball from the elk's pen. Then they killed the elk.

In 1936, a horse kicked an older boy named Charles Crowell after he was placed out on a farm near Northfield, and he died at the University of Minnesota Hospital shortly thereafter. They brought him back for his funeral in the school chapel, and six former classmates acted as pallbearers. The senior chorus sang "Abide With Me" and "Whispering Hope," and a boys' quartet marked the sad occasion at the cemetery by singing, "The Old Rugged Cross." We children, who witnessed these tragedies, simply sucked up the sadness and marched on.

45

In late 1934, when Oscar and I were 8 and 7 years old, the matron called us into a room and told us she had a letter that she wanted to read to us. The news was that our mother had died in the TB sanatorium. I can't remember the matron consoling us or giving us any kind words, but our mother's death didn't affect us very much. By now we had little or no memory of her. We had been so young when she went away three or four years earlier, and we had not seen her or heard news about her. Circumstances beyond our control had affected the details and setting of our lives during those years, and we had adjusted to and accepted our situation as the new norm. Life went on.

After Mr. Merrill died, Mendus Vevle was named the new superintendent. To my knowledge, Mr. Vevle never laid a hand on a child. The image of the institution was very important to him. If he had a weakness, it was that he didn't keep a closer eye on what was actually going on inside the cottages. He put full trust in the longtime matrons, and they could sway him.

I had a personal experience to support my criticism of Mr. Vevle. During our recreation time, we were absolutely not allowed to leave our C-11 playground to go anywhere else—especially over to Mr. Vevle's office in the Main Building. But I wanted to be transferred to C-3 where Oscar was, so I mustered my courage one day and went over to talk to the superintendent. He listened politely and led me to believe it would be possible to transfer.

I ran back to our C-11 playground, and in less than ten minutes Miss Morgan called me inside. Screaming, she asked how I dared leave the playground, go to Mr. Vevle's office, and request a transfer.

She ended her tirade with, "You will NOT be transferred to C-3." Obviously Miss Morgan, not Mr. Vevle, had the final word. It broke my heart.

Each evening thereafter, before going to sleep, I would silently say "The Lord's Prayer" followed by "Now I lay me down to sleep. I pray thee Lord my soul to keep. If I should die before I wake, I pray thee Lord my soul to take. This I ask for Jesus' sake, amen." Then I added, "Please, God, transfer me to C-3."

I continued that same plea to God for two years. Then one day Miss Morgan notified me that I was being transferred, not to C-3, but to C-16. My plea to God to join my brother in C-3 continued. Finally, after about a year in C-16, Miss Steele told me to collect my belongings. My prayer had finally been answered. However, after the transfer I continued my prayer. After a few weeks I realized what I was doing and told myself, "Harvey, you ARE in C-3."

That incident taught me two lessons. One is that many times we pray habitually, without thought or meaning, and the other is that God does answer prayers, but in his own time. Sometimes the answer is "no." God knew I wasn't mature enough yet to live in C-3, and I thank him for his wisdom.

In the fall we seventh and eighth grade boys were excused from school to pick potatoes on our school farm. On our way out there, three of us got a little frisky and jumped off the wagon. We were heading to the dump to execute some rats with our slingshots.

When the gardener noticed we were missing, he knew right away where we had gone. Bringing us back to the potato field, he made us strip down, and in front of all the other kids, he gave us a whipping with the horse reins. He wanted everyone to know that he was the man in charge. Yes, he got that point across!

Our horse barn housed about ten teams of quality workhorses and many ponies for lighter work. I'll always remember "Pop" Behrends, a guy we all liked, driving around the grounds with his little wagon pulled by two ponies. He picked up garbage at every facility. During my stay, both the horse and cow barns burned down in spectacular fires. I can remember seeing dead cows after the fire, still in their stanchions.

Although I recall many experiences that were laced with conflict, tragedy and disappointment, some very good times stand out vividly too. One proud moment came when Governor Harold Stassen visited the school. I shook his hand in front of the gym. My proudest moment, however, occurred at the Spring Athletic Banquet in 1943. Voted by my peers, I was named the winner of the Superintendent's Cup Trophy, an annual award given to the year's most outstanding athlete. What a privilege it was to have my name engraved on this trophy, added to the likes of Clifford Jarchow, Vernon Lowry, Victor Tiensuu, Orville Beuthien, Donovan Knapp and James Barron, my heroes of previous years.

These are two more picture post cards. They may have been sent to family by State Schoolers or kept as souvenirs. The building above is the new school that I watched them build in 1933.

Boys learned woodworking and girls took domestic science in seventh and eighth grades. Today our museum displays several woodworking pieces and a basket made by State School boys.

From time to time somebody would line us up, point us into the sun and take our picture, which most of us didn't appear to care too much about. These are C-11 boys, and I am in the front row with my eyes shut.

Three of my pals: Gene, Abraham, myself and Russel

During spring and summer, we did what boys everywhere did; we played baseball. All our sports were fiercely competitive, and what our teams lacked in depth they more than made up for in hustle. Ball games were exciting as boys from one cottage played against the team from another cottage.

There were three times more boys than girls at the State School, but this is pretty much how the girls of my era dressed and looked in their school clothes. They all hated their clunky shoes.

With adult supervision, we boys kept the campus mowed, raked and trimmed. I definitely preferred baseball to landscaping.

Because of our shared experience at the State School, Oscar was not only a brother, but a best friend. My oldest sister Hazel kept in touch, and she visited us three times and took these pictures. One time she even brought Dad, Ruth, and Ruben.

These are the boys from C-8. There is some bravado and rebellion conveyed in these photos, as we are starting to look a little more like young men and a little less like kids.

These are typical older boys, teenagers who are nearing the age when they will be moving out into the world beyond the school.

Running Away

Many kids ran away from the State School, especially during summertime. Kids ran away for adventure, excitement and to find their real homes. Most often authorities found them and returned them within a day or two. Those who were gone for more than three days had to return to the Detention Cottage for a three-week stay in case they picked up anything contagious. Boys who repeatedly ran away were reassigned to Red Wing Reform School. Some made a successful run, never to return.

An Owatonna man I knew ran away from the State School when he was a kid in the 1920s. I always wondered why he had so much trouble with his feet. One day his son told me that his father had run away from the State School and froze his feet so badly that it left him crippled for life. He chose the wrong time of the year.

I ran away four times--just for something to do. Planning a getaway was fun. It gave me something to brag about. On the outside I would swagger, but on the inside I wanted to be caught, and I ran just fast enough so that catching me was not too difficult. I always remember the advice of an older boy who said, "Don't go too far south. You'll end up on a chain gang." One autumn night two of us crawled out a window and ran. We had barely started out the next morning when we came to some tall grass near the institution, a great cover, we thought. We were not aware that it was hunting season, but all of a sudden we saw two men approaching with guns raised. Scared to death, we jumped up, and much to our surprise the hunters were two State School employees.

Seeing us they yelled, "Get the hell out of here and back on the grounds. We're checking when we get back to see if you're in the cottage." With our tails between our legs, we took off running as fast as we could and joined the kids for breakfast.

Let's set the stage for another escape. It's the late '30s. I'm almost 12 years old, and as far as my memory serves me, I've rarely been off the State School grounds. The incomparable Brown Bomber, Joe Louis, is Heavyweight Champion of the World. The rest of my heroes aren't doing so well though. Capone is in Alcatraz, Dillinger was killed by cops outside a theater in Chicago, Baby Face Nelson and Machine Gun Kelly have also received their comeuppance. These were men who could look authority straight in the face and spit in his eye--our kind of men!

Three of us decided that a man could only take so much. Enough was enough. We weren't taking any more. We were breaking out. The institution hadn't been built that could hold us. So deep in the bowels of Cottage 11, we set our plans in motion. All winter the planning went on, day after day. We'd make our escape in the spring, and our plans would leave no room for error. This adventure wasn't for the faint of heart; it called for nerves of steel. This was the real world--not kid stuff. It was the big time! Get ready world, three shrewd desperadoes are coming right at you. May and warm weather finally arrived as we took care of last-minute preparations. We gave our marbles to our best friends and readied our slingshots. I gave a note to a friend to slip to Pauline in C-5. "I'm sorry, but I have to go. I'll miss seeing you in the dining room, but it's better this way. Maybe someday...."

The moment of truth came that night. As the others slept, we crawled out one of the basement windows, ran through the orchard and worked our way down to the railroad tracks. There we lay in the grass waiting for the 4 a.m. freight going east, just as we had planned. I was thinking that I would never again hear some big-mouth start the day by shouting, "Rise and shine! Daylight in the swamps!" Ah, I was free.

Before the train rumbled into sight, we could hear its lonesome whistle cry. My mouth became cotton dry, my muscles tensed. Our positioning was perfect. The train screeched to a noisy stop with an open door right there in front of us. Wait a minute! All of a sudden the train looked so big and frightening.

We spoke not a word. After a few minutes the iron monster jerked violently and headed east. Frozen with fear, we three desperadoes watched it disappear into the eastern horizon, and not one of us made a move.

Well, now what? We decided to walk the rails west--they must lead to somewhere. Shortly after daybreak, we entered the outskirts of a place called Meriden. A lady above a grocery store called down and invited us in for breakfast.

Well, why not? Even when you're on the run, you have to eat. And what a breakfast it was, with eggs, toast, and jelly! We thought we were in heaven imagining the guys back at the school eating the same old mush like they had every other morning. The lady sure liked to talk, but she was a good cook.

We started thinking it was time to move on. But all of a sudden Mr. Doleman, the state agent, walked in and said, "You're goin' home boys!" Hmmm.....How did he know we were here? Hey, wait a minute. Do you think that nice lady could have ratted on us? She did leave the room once, but she seemed so nice!

By 9 a.m. we were back in C-11. By 9:10 we were standing in the corner waiting to be dealt with in the proper fashion, a technique designed to deter us from even thinking about future escapes. I don't remember a severe punishment for that particular transgression, although I've heard stories from others who were severely punished for running away. Our matron mockingly asked us if we had seen the streetcars and skyscrapers. Gosh, I thought, we must not have gotten that far into town because I didn't see any skyscrapers. But I decided right then and there that I'd someday go back to the town of Meriden to see those skyscrapers. And at the noon meal, I shyly smiled at my Pauline. Well, at least she wouldn't have to face the future alone.

The Unspoken Word, "Sex"

Was there sexual activity at the State School? Is the world round? Sex has ruined careers and marriages, caused murders, and brought the President of the United States to an impeachment. Sex is one of the strongest forces in the universe.

Of course there was sex at the State School, but rest assured, those in authority never discussed it. You can't house large groups of teenagers in close quarters and expect them to keep apart. No matter the challenges and risks, they will figure out a way to follow natural instinct.

There was also sex among employees. Sometimes a kid would walk into a room and see something we weren't supposed to see. We had some young, unmarried teachers and employees who had some trysts.

There were also sexual incidents between adults and children. Donna Scott Norling, in her 1996 book *Patty's Journey,* describes lying in her little bed when she was about 5 years old and pretending she was hovering at the ceiling as she was being molested by a custodian. When the unwritten code of an institution forbids snitching on other children or adults, adults find it extremely easy to get away with victimizing children.

The ratio of boys to girls was about 3-1. Consequently several boys probably had a crush on one girl. My first crushes were on Pauline Lutz and Miss Cahill, my fourth grade teacher. Of course, these crushes were one-sided and produced nothing like a kiss or even a squeeze. The most I could ever hope for was a wistful glance, accompanied by the feeling of wasted love, and I certainly didn't understand much about those feelings of attraction.

When I was about 8 years old, I had a strange relationship with one of the older boys. I didn't really like him, yet I did. It was odd, but I was like his stooge. I felt important when he let me hang around him, and I would do anything he asked of me.

One day on the playground he made me sit with my penis outside my pants as other kids played around me. He would humiliate me, and I would take it for some inexplicable reason. I still remember it vividly and hate the memory. I never saw him after I left the school.

My first sexual experience took place in C-11. One of the older boys crawled in bed with me. He masturbated me. He repeated this a couple of times, and I never said a word to anyone.

He was placed out, and a couple of years later he wrote a letter back to the institution. It was pinned on the bulletin board in the Main Building. It was difficult to read the letter because, as he explained, he had lost his right arm in a farm accident. He was learning to write with his left hand. In the letter he said that he thought God had punished him for something he did at the State School. As I read it, I knew exactly what he was getting at. I wonder how many other boys he was involved with.

Before tractors we had work horses. One of the workers on our farm, Merle, had to hire a stud horse for the mare.

Merle said, "Here, Harvey, I'll show you something you won't see in the movies." We went behind the barn and watched the proceedings.

We had a guy we called Moose--a big kid, a few years older than I was. Mr. Vevle, our superintendent, was an equestrian, and Moose got caught screwing one of Mr. Vevle's horses. Moose was so ashamed that he never again went to the dining room because he couldn't face all those curious eyes. Someone delivered his meals to his cottage. He was later captured in Bataan and survived the death march, held as prisoner of war by the Japanese for the entire war. He died in Texas at a Veterans' hospital, a beaten man from years of captivity.

A married employee was having an affair with my fifth grade teacher, who was single. I'm sure most of the employees knew about it because my former matron Julia Keefe told me about it many years later. Both employees were called into the Superintendent's office and told that it they didn't knock it off, they'd both be fired. That ended the romance.

I didn't know it at the time, but later I learned that occasionally girls would get pregnant and would be sent to Sauk Centre State Home School for Girls. They sure didn't get pregnant by themselves. Teenage boys and girls who worked in the basement service center beneath the dining room found lots of corners and crevices.

By the time most boys and girls were 15 or 16 years old, a couple of years before their termination as Wards of the State and before they graduated from high school, they would be placed out on indenture contracts. One reason was that they were big and strong enough to be helpful elsewhere, but another objective may have been to thin out the number of teenagers on that small campus who undoubtedly had raging hormones and natural urges. Of course there was sex. Why wouldn't there be?

Matrons, My Surrogate Mothers

The severity of punishment, an integral part of daily life at the State School, depended on the cottage the child lived in. It was all up to the matron who made rules that dictated the atmosphere. Here's a true story told me by one of the teachers at the school. One week after the institution changed over to a school for retarded children in 1945, a kid ran away and walked into the Governor's office and told him how he and the other kids were being treated. In a matter of a few days, every employee had been warned that they were putting their jobs in jeopardy if they laid a hand on those kids. Obviously retarded children were not accustomed to the kind of harsh treatment that was commonplace for us orphans.

One of the cornerstones of the State School was: "Family-like life in cottages. The cottages are the homes, and are under the care of intelligent women who assume the relation of mothers to the children. The hope is that the child will live in the cottage less than a year."

Intelligent? I don't know about that. Only one was college educated to my knowledge. These women certainly didn't have mothering skills. I lived under the direction of five matrons during my eleven years at the school, and with the exception of one, they were unaware or insensitive to a child's needs. My five matrons were middle-aged, single women who had never married or had children of their own. They lived in the cottage twenty-four hours a day, seven days a week, and they rarely took vacations or got involved with anything outside the State School.

I was too young to remember Miss Moriarity in C-12, the Detention Cottage, but I've been told several times that when a child who was crying arrived, Miss Moriarity slapped him or her across the face and said, "We don't cry here."

Eva Carlson Jensen, in her book, *No Tears Allowed,* writes, "I started to cry, and I said, 'I want my mama.' A lady came over to me and slapped me across the face so hard I saw stars. She said, 'There will be no crying here.'" Today, at age 90, Eva still cannot cry.

Miss White, the matron in C-6, the small boys' cottage, was a quaint, strange lady. I have no vivid memories of her, but I believe she was generally pleasant. I do recall an assistant matron, who took away my marbles. She told me she would give them to some children who would really appreciate them-- her own children. That hurt.

When I was 6 years old, I moved to C-11, a cottage for boys age 6 to 14. Miss Morgan was the matron, and in my opinion, she had no more business being in charge of children than I have of being the pope. She raised children in an atmosphere of loveless, unreasonable discipline and regimentation, as opposed to the environment in which children should be raised.

During my eight years in Cottage 11, discipline never changed. Miss Morgan ruled the cottage with an iron hand, and her favorite comment was, "What's that smart remark from a broken dish?" I don't think modern educators would approve of an adult referring to a child in such a demeaning way. Slapping was a daily occurrence, and when that didn't work, the radiator brush came out. Miss Morgan could handle her own punishments. Matrons who were not so physically fit would jot down the names of offenders during the week, and on Saturday morning they would call in one of the men to administer the lickin'.

Besides getting slapped, I remember two beatings from Miss Morgan that crossed the line. One day as I was going down to the basement, I made the mistake of saying under my breath, "Oh, shut up." She heard me and went for the radiator brush. The beating she gave me was so savage that I was bruised for weeks on my back and arms. The other time she beat me because I took off my necktie as I was walking to school. We were the only cottage whose matron made the boys wear ties, so when we got to school the other kids made fun of us and called us sissies. She noticed me taking off my tie as she stood outside the cottage door, called me back, and beat my head against a cement wall so viciously I thought she was going to kill me. I've resisted wearing neckties all my adult life.

We certainly weren't mollycoddled. By today's standards, we boys, under Miss Morgan in C-11, were abused emotionally, mentally, socially, spiritually and physically. She was the primary adult in our lives who modeled how adults treat children and humiliate them, an adult authority figure who abused kids and got away with it year after year. Her behavior affected how many of her charges treated others when they grew up. I spent eight formative years under these conditions.

Miss Morgan had a dog named Pal. It was a nice dog, but we hated Pal because she treated him like royalty while she abused us kids. Once in awhile the dog would run off, and we loved that because Miss Morgan would allow us to leave the playground to look for it. We would run the railroad tracks and woods behind the power plant, hoping we'd never find the critter. We loved playing in the woods and near the tracks because we so seldom enjoyed any freedom.

One day we found the dog dead. Rumor was that it had been poisoned, but I can't testify to that. We brought it back, and Miss Morgan made us conduct a funeral for Pal in the woods, then bury it. We were tickled by some kind of perverse revenge because the person who had been so mean to us was suffering. It was hard to act heart broken at Pal's funeral and burial.

Miss Morgan was a stickler for enforcing the rule that we could never venture off our small playground. And when we went out to play, everyone went out, and nobody came back in until everybody came back. It didn't matter if you had to go to the bathroom or if you were cold or sick. The rule was firm, as were all her rules. There was no negotiating.

In addition to her other acts of cruelty, Miss Morgan was great at humiliating children. I'm not sure why I was selected as the representative from Cottage 11, but each Sunday I had to take the bus into town to Trinity Lutheran Church. A few of us were herded in at the last minute in front of the entire congregation, which was humiliating, and led to a room where we could neither see nor hear the pastor. While I was in church and hating it, the rest of the kids were out playing. Then, when I got back to the cottage, the boys were lined up to march to dinner. Every Sunday Miss Morgan asked me the same question, "Harvey, tell us what you learned in church today."

I would have loved to have had a good answer, but since I hadn't heard or seen the pastor, I squirmed and meekly said, "I don't know."

Her response was always the same. "Then why are you going to church?" Right then and there I vowed I would never go to church when I got old enough to determine such things for myself. It has taken nearly a lifetime to recover from this spiritual abuse.

Being raised in that cottage ruined many lives. It was an incubator that would lead men to lives of crime, depression, addiction and suicide. I am personally aware that of my childhood friends who lived with me in Cottage 11, two hung themselves in prison, one escaped from Stillwater Prison and was shot down by police, another was gunned down in his apartment, one had a mental breakdown, one has completely blocked out his past, and four are alcoholic (including myself). Now, think about it. Were all these children born bad? I don't think so.

Many years after I grew to be an adult, a teacher told me, "We knew there was something strange going on in the cottages." After a short hesitation she added, "But what could we do?"

It is difficult to recall times when Miss Morgan showed kindness or compassion, but I do remember her showing compassion the evening before Herman Topping was scheduled to have an appendectomy. She asked us to pray for him. Dr. Arvid Antroinen, who lived in C-11 in the 1920s, recalled her fondly. "I was her pet," he said. My brother Oscar remembers that a former State Schooler came back for a visit. He was down and almost out. Miss Morgan harbored him in the cottage and brought him meals from the dining room.

But the vast majority of the stories about Miss Morgan that most of the boys of my generation repeat whenever we have reunions are negative. At the dedication ceremony in 1993, when we unveiled the statues, I renewed acquaintances with an old friend who spent years in C-11 with me. We were standing in front of the building, two men of retirement age, and I asked him, "Well, Milt, after all these years, what do you think of Morgan now?"

Looking towards the cottage he answered, "She was the meanest person I ever met in my life. If she were alive today, I'd probably kill her."

Finally, after eight years, I was transferred to C-16, a "big boys' cottage." I had to find a new comfort zone, but that was to be expected. Life was more comfortable here, and we had more freedom. Miss Steele, the matron, had a drinking problem. We all knew it because it was obvious, but it was okay. She was stern but not harsh or mean. We worked in the fields, shoveled sidewalks, mowed lawns and enjoyed playing on a bigger playground. I graduated from knickers to long pants, a sure sign that I was now a big boy.

When I was 15, my prayer was answered and I was finally transferred to C-3, called the "mean boys' cottage." The atmosphere was different, and there was no pecking order. The boys were more mature, and I was assigned to work in the dairy barn.

Merle Indvik was the head herdsman, and he came to C-3 at 4 a.m. to wake us. Some of the boys went to work in the bakery, and others went to the dairy barn. On my first morning in the dairy barn, I stood and watched as a couple of experienced boys went out to the pasture to get the cows. I watched in amazement as the cows walked into the barn and in an orderly fashion went to their stanchions. I thought that was pretty neat.

The next morning the same thing happened. I asked one of the kids, "Do they go into the same stanchions every day?" When he assured me that they did, I thought, "That's really something!" The reality was that the cows were no different from the children. We were just like robots. When you're institutionalized, you do what you're trained to do without ever thinking.

My first job in the barn was shoveling manure. It made me sick to my stomach, and I vomited, but after a couple of days I got used to it. Next Merle got me started milking a cow by hand as I sat on a three-legged stool. How I remember those swishing tails in my face.

Then a miracle happened. The State School invested in their first Hinman milking machines. While the machine took care of most of the milking chore, we boys still had to strip the last milk from the cows. We also had to milk the ones with warts on their udders, since the machines could not be used on them.

After milking each cow, we would take the pails and weigh each cow's output. One morning as I was walking with my pail full of milk to be weighed, one of the kids who had always been taunting me tripped me from behind.

I wheeled around and hit him flush on the jaw. He and his pail of milk went sprawling all over the cement floor behind the cows. Merle was standing right there. My first thought was that he would punish me for my actions. Instead, he acted like nothing had happened. Then he walked up to me and said, "Good for you. I was wondering how long you were going to take that crap." I felt ten feet tall.

Working in the dairy barn was hard work for me. I enjoyed myself however, and I think I was Merle's fair-haired boy. For the first time in my life, I felt special. And then Miss Keefe, my new matron, arrived on the scene.

Julia A. Keefe

When she entered C-3 for the first time, thirty pairs of anxious eyes watched her every step. Somebody has to be kidding. This won't even be a challenge. She looked so fragile with thin legs, gray hair, glasses, fifty-ish. She seemed out of place. Intimidated? Oh yes, I'm sure. It was her first day on the job at the State School as head matron of C-3, a boys' cottage known as the "mean boys' cottage."

She told me years later that other employees had told her she wouldn't last a week over there. They were wrong. She was there to say good-bye to all thirty boys as they went out into the world, one by one. And she kept in touch with many of them for many years.

During World War II, she instituted a newspaper for State Public School alumni. Because of this paper, I found a sailor from the school on board the *USS Randolph*, the ship that took me overseas. She typed and mailed this paper to State School servicemen all over the world. This was a remarkable thing to do, as we were all hungry for mail during the war years.

My brother and I visited this lady until the day she died in a New Brighton rest home at age 92. I'm sure the employees thought we were her sons because she always introduced us as her boys. We loved her very much.

The lady wasn't out to change the world, but in her value system, she realized authority wasn't always right. She knew the treatment a young boy received would affect him in the future. She realized the love you give a child will last forever.

You won't find this lady's name on the lists of rich and famous, but if success is measured by sensitivity and sound, practical judgment, the name Julia A. Keefe will be right at the top.

Keefe was also wise enough to know that red-blooded American boys will be mischievous on occasion, and that doesn't make them bad. Boys being boys wasn't going to change the course of history. She had the capacity to know you can't continually oppress growing boys, so she let us express ourselves. She let us win once in awhile. The institution's rules were simply too rigid. She made her own rules, simply because to her they made more sense. Her iconoclastic attitude was like a breath of fresh air.

Julia Keefe was a woman of principle backed with action. For example, she did the unthinkable; she invited us into her living quarters, let us read her newspaper, listen to her radio or just sit. We were always welcome. Her door was always open, and she trusted us. Not overnight, but soon disciplining was at a minimum. We policed each other, and she made more than one trip to the superintendent's office on our behalf. She fought for us, we knew it, and we respected and loved her for her ethics. We were from C-3, and we were Jule Keefe's boys!

Eventually, it was no longer "Miss Keefe." It was--are you ready?--just Jule. I visited her for a couple of years after I left the school, and these visits are noted in my records that were filed by my social worker, Miss Emma Nelson. Sometimes a couple of us would stop in after playing sports and merely visit with her, and other times we would play cards.

Occasionally we'd have lunch with her, and she described me to Miss Nelson as an appreciative, well-mannered and well-behaved boy. She believed I was keeping reasonable hours, and she thought I had made great progress and improvement. It was refreshing to have someone stand up for me, and her positive opinion and kind words undoubtedly affected me for the better.

Years after my brother and I had left the school, I arrogantly told her that we used to pull one over on her once in awhile. She looked at me, smiled, and said, "You mean when you used to put those pillows in your bed and sneak down the fire escape?" Since she was no dummy, she knew all the time, but she realized that those little victories over the immutable rules and regulations of our institution were important to us.

In all her dealings with youngsters at the school, to my knowledge she only had one bad experience. Later the boy involved ended his life in prison.

A professional teacher who excelled in music, Julia A. Keefe moved into a world that was foreign to her. By sheer decency, she conquered the hearts of supposedly unmanageable boys. She touched every one of us in a very special way.

Jule's interest in us was sincere. It lasted long after we left the State School. She liked to keep track of what we were doing, who we married, and how our families were doing. One evening she took three or four of us to Gallivan's, one of St. Paul's finest restaurants. Her order to the waitress was curt. "Give the boys anything they want." She was like a mother hen, as proud as she could be. She was with her boys, and wanted everybody to know it.

Julia Keefe was one of a kind, and that's too bad. We could have used more like her. A few years ago I talked to Emil Haugen, a childhood friend who lived with me in both C-11 and C-3. Emil was then the director of a large YMCA in Michigan. I asked Emil what he thought of Jule Keefe after all these years, and his answer was, "Julia Keefe was an island of tranquility in a stormy sea."

Of all the adults who were hired to take care of me and teach me at the State School, Julia Keefe was the most skilled and the most successful. Her kindness, wisdom and understanding really made a difference in my life, and I will always think of her as a parent figure.

Julia Keefe at the door of C-3, the "mean boys' cottage."

Assistant matron Gorven with me (left) and my friend Billy, Miss White, my first matron in the small boys' cottage, and a matron with boys from an earlier era, dressed in their Sunday best.

Golden Gloves Boxing Program

Every year in January and February I get sentimental when I think back to when boxing was king in Owatonna. That old armory was dangerously packed for three nights of exciting boxing action when the Golden Gloves tournament took place. My wife tells me that on those nights her dad milked their cows early because nothing could stop him and her brother from seeing the fights.

The Golden Gloves program sponsored tournaments all over the country in those days, but none were better than the tournament in Owatonna, sponsored and run by the Junior Chamber of Commerce. I was proud to be a part of it. Over the years I would see Joe Shea, Don Bruno, Bob Jurgensen, Louie Allgeyer or Stan Johnson, and the first thing that would come to my mind was the Golden Gloves program. It was a very special time in my life, and it was a very big event for the State School, which was my home.

With football season finished, boxing training would start in the south wing of the State School gym. There were many cut lips, blackened eyes and bloody noses during the course of the training months. Training centers today require headgear, but we never knew those things existed. Just lace the gloves on, and let's go. Each evening we would work out--some of us skilled, and others not so skilled, but all with fighting hearts. I used to think some of the guys were born fighting. Often our toughest fights were against our friends during training.

Matches involving State School boxers made up a major part of the Owatonna tournament. When a State Schooler was in the ring, it was never dull. Other participants from this region came from as far south as New Richland to as far north as Northfield, and from Dodge Center to Waseca and all points between. At that time, there were only eight weight classes.

The first year the State School participated, seven of its boxers were crowned champions. Year after year, until the school closed, we walked off with the team trophy. If this sounds like boasting, it's only because I am. I was and still am proud of the State School guys.

Because of the war in later years, the school didn't have a coach. All able-bodied men between the ages of 18 and 37 had answered the call to fight for their country. To fill the vacancy, the gardener stepped in to fill the void. I loved Tom, and I say this respectfully. A boxing genius he was not, but he gave generously of his time, was a good disciplinarian and organizer, and he knew how to get us ready.

We weren't exactly pros--especially at some of the intangibles like taking off weight. One of our fighters had a couple of pounds to lose at the afternoon weigh-in, and Ex-lax was his answer. That night when they called his name to enter the ring he couldn't answer the bell because he was answering a more urgent call.

Another night, we brought down our own gloves. When the fights ended, we noticed they were 10-ounce instead of the sanctioned 12-ounce gloves. We scored a few knockouts that night, and the gloves remained a State School secret.

Another incident I remember happened between rounds of a fight. In an attempt to encourage one of our guys who was taking a beating, Tom told our fighter he was doing great, that the other guy wasn't touching him. The fighter looked up at Tom and said, "Then you better check the referee because somebody out there is beating the hell out of me."

Cummings, Benecke, Tenhoff, Jackovich, Hoffman, Donoso, the Ronglien brothers and Smokie Cloud were familiar State School names. The Dudleys of Northfield and Huntingtons of Waseca, Boecke, Anhorn and Jandro and Morris were popular names in the Golden Gloves circle. There were no headlines, cheerleaders or banners. We fought for pride and brought home a little medal if we were good enough.

I loved the Golden Gloves program. Besides meeting a lot of nice people outside the State School, I gained recognition as a State School boxer, and I liked that. It made me feel good about myself. I fought in five Golden Gloves tournaments, besides fighting during the off-season on other fight cards, which earned me up to $20.

In the first tournament, I lost my first bout. In the next three tournaments, I got beat in the finals. In my final tournament, I fought at 145 pounds. I won my first three fights to advance to the finals.

My fight was the final fight of the night, and was regarded as the headliner. I was in top shape and feeling good about myself as we got our instructions in the center of the ring before we returned to our corners awaiting the sound of the bell.

When the bell rang, I danced to the center of the ring, eager to get on with it, and my opponent was there to meet me. I made a feint to his right, and as I moved left, he drove a powerful left to my body that bent me over.

He stepped back momentarily as I gasped for air, and I recovered and moved in for a hard left and not so hard right. He parried both blows and made a counter attack, firing off a flurry of punches so convincingly that the referee stepped in and stopped the battle of the century, declaring it a mismatch. That was the end of my not so spectacular fighting career.

My opponent was Raul Donoso from New Richland, a former State Schooler and good friend. He went on to win the prestigious Northwest Golden Gloves Tournament and advanced to the Chicago tournament, where he won two fights. While winning the second fight, he broke his hand and had to be disqualified.

Raul fought in the Korean War and later became a minister. I didn't hear from Raul for many years. One night in the 1990s, around 9 p.m., I got a call from the state of Washington. It was Raul, and we talked for three hours. I've heard from him a few more times, and he's now retired.

In my opinion, Golden Gloves did more for the self-esteem of State School participants than anything else at the school. The benefits of the program were twofold. Boxing gave the community good entertainment, a winter break unmatched today. For the participants, Golden Gloves taught lessons in life, and gave us personal satisfaction and a moment of glory. I'm proud that I was privileged to be a part of it.

Minorities and Discrimination

I'm often asked if we had children of minority races and nationalities at the State School, and were they discriminated against. Yes, we had black children, Indian children. Old photographs and a silent film someone found a few years ago show racial diversity. To the best of my recollection, we children did not discriminate or harass kids because of their race or nationality. We all lived and played together without thinking much about it. However, it should come as no surprise to learn that members of the State School staff and other people in town did practice discrimination.

The practice of separatism in American life is a historical fact, and Minnesotans practiced it right along with everyone else. Whether they defined or distinguished themselves by religion, national origin, wealth, education, social standing, political belief or race, most people held themselves apart from those with different backgrounds or views and made some effort to exclude or discriminate against others. Mixed marriage between members of different religions was a big deal, and *any* kind of business or social alliance between members of different races was a huge deal.

It doesn't matter whether we call it discrimination or racism; the important thing is that treating members of minority races and nationalities differently was part of our lives. The KKK was active in Minnesota, even in small towns, and members of minority groups felt the effect. Remember, Jackie Robinson didn't break baseball's color barrier until 1947, and it wasn't until 1964, a century after the end of the Civil War, that Congress passed the Civil Rights Act.

With that in mind, let's consider how members of minorities were treated at the State School. Peter Razor says in his book, *While the Locust Slept,* that some staff members called him "Injun" and that he felt put down. I can remember other Indian children named Smokey Cloud, Bernard Landro, Cecil and Art Ankerstrom.

Noel Moran was a light colored boy of mixed race who came to the State School as a baby and spent his entire childhood there. I heard, and it may have been true, that the reason he was placed there as an infant was that he was mixed race. Noel, who had movie star looks, was a top athlete at Owatonna High School and very popular.

While in high school, he started shining around State School Superintendent Vevle's daughter. Mr. Vevle called Noel's matron, Louise Shimpach, into his office and told her to tell Noel that he was a black man and that he should therefore stay away from his daughter. Louise, who told me this story herself, told him that dealing with this issue wasn't her job and that the State School officials should have told Noel when he was little that he was black.

Mr. Vevle told Louise that she had to either deal with telling Noel or lose her job. Louise got along well with Noel and didn't want to upset him, but with the superintendent's choice confronting her, she called Noel in, and in the best way she could, told him he was black. Noel reacted violently to the news, threw his chair against the wall and called Louise a lying bitch. He stormed out of the room and never spoke another word to her. It broke Louise's heart because she liked and respected Noel.

After high school graduation, Noel stayed on at the State School as an employee. Then, as the drums of war started to beat louder and louder, and war with Germany and Japan became a reality, Noel joined the Army. The military at that time was segregated, and to Noel's utter amazement, he was put in a black unit. He did well, survived the war and received an honorable discharge.

After discharge, on his way to California, Noel was determined to make a stop in Owatonna. Louise Shimpach was sitting in a chair looking out her living room window at 215 East Pearl when, to her surprise, a taxicab stopped in front of her house. A man in military uniform stepped out, walked to her house, and rang the doorbell.

Louise opened the door, and to her astonishment, she looked into the eyes of Noel Moran. She invited him in. He said, "Louise, I'm so sorry. I just couldn't believe I was black until I got into the Army. Forgive me for my actions. I'm on my way to California, but I had to stop and apologize to you. I plan to get married, but I promise you I will never have children." And he never did. He became a police officer and died at the age of 52.

The fact that Noel's race was so shameful and regrettable to him tells a lot about attitudes at that time. John Cummings, another black kid, was quite a guy. He boxed in the Golden Gloves and was a star football, basketball and baseball player for Owatonna High School. One day he played on the baseball team and then quickly changed into his track uniform to star on the track team.

After leaving the State School, John lived at the Owatonna Fire Hall, where he served as a volunteer fireman. He moved to St. Paul and worked for many years as a bartender. He married and had a family.

John was one of the nicest people I ever met. One night my brother Oscar and I were on a bus going to some fights in St. Paul. As we were going down a street, in surprise, I yelled to Oscar, "There's Cummings!"

I hadn't seen him in years, but because of our Golden Gloves experience at the State School, I thought he was probably going to the fights too. Oscar and I went in and sat down with an eye to the entrance. Sure enough, in walks Cummings. He saw us, and we had a great time. That night he told us of being taunted on the high school football field by opposing players, often using the "n" word. This really bothered him to the point where he chose to sit out one Big Nine conference game. John died of a heart attack a few years ago.

Blacky Anderson and Earl Pettiford, two other black kids, played on the Owatonna High School football team in the late 1930s. If I knew Blacky's real first name I'd use it here to avoid censure, but I don't really know what it was. Butch Hertz, the Owatonna High School athletic director who coached football, basketball and baseball at that time, told me years later, "I don't know what we would have done if it weren't for the State School kids." In fact, he went on to say that State Schoolers and their athletic talents were a big reason Owatonna got into the Big Nine Conference.

On the other side of the coin, I can understand why residents of Owatonna had mixed feelings about State School athletes. Because the State School was so self-contained, the talent of State Schoolers was more or less kept under wraps until they emerged into the public school as high school freshmen. Local kids often expressed animosity when they were beat out by a State Schooler for a position they thought they had earned and worked for, and I can fully understand their resentment. A kid would play with his schoolmates for years through the grades, thinking he would be starting at a certain position in a high school sport. Then along came a boy from the State School who beat him out. As a parent, I wouldn't have liked that either, but such was the situation.

Although I didn't personally know him, former State Schooler Henry Brown, the only black man in Owatonna during the 1930s and '40s, became a legend. Henry had stayed on in Owatonna after leaving the State School and worked at the post office. Henry was a wonderful man and soloist who shared his vocal talent with members of the First Baptist Church and with the community. He is remembered for his stirring rendition of "God Bless America," and we were privileged to include a recording of this in our documentary we made about the orphanage, *The Children Remember, Life at the Minnesota State Public School for Dependent and Neglected Children.*

A Boy From C-11

This is my official Golden Gloves photo, taken around 1945.

Noel Moran, despite his accomplishments in sports and movie star looks, was a victim of social attitudes toward people of mixed race.

State School Boys' 1939-1940 Basketball Team: Front: Lenny Hedahl, John Cummings, Vernon Lowry, Vic Laskowski, Bill Reynolds, Norris Houlm Back: Ralph Benecke, Dan Zigich, Vic Tiensuu, Orville Beuthien, Nick Zigich. (11 wins, 1 loss)

Being Placed Out

The fourth cornerstone of the State School was placing children out, on adoption or by another arrangement. "If possible, the dependent children, after their basic training, will be placed out (adopted, fostered or indentured) preferably in rural homes. State agents will be responsible for selecting suitable homes for the children, and for annual inspection thereafter of such placements."

To assist with that goal, the school employed state agents who lived at or near the school. The agents were to become personally acquainted with the children in order to better match them up with families. The other half of their job required them to travel the state to secure applications from families who wanted children. In the early days of the school, agents traveled by train and horse-drawn wagons. Later automobiles made their jobs much easier. After a child was matched with a family, the agent would visit the child at least once every year, or more often if they felt it necessary.

From the beginning adoption was the number one choice for placement. However, adoption never happened in a big way. A second solution met with greater success, the Indenture Contract. An original Indenture Contract document is on display in the State School Museum. Very similar to slavery, this contract between the state and a family said the family agreed to provide the child with kind treatment in the family, at least four months of education per year until age 18, training in some useful occupation, and at the expiration of the contract (age 18), the child was to be given $75 to $100 and two suits of clothing.

While some families met these conditions, more often than not quite the opposite was true. Children were usually taken solely for work. Few were made to feel a part of the family or were given any payment or other compensation for their labors.

To get around the education requirement, many sent the child to school for one day in each of four months and called that meeting the education requirement. As for training in a useful occupation, that occupation usually was simply farming for boys and housemaid/farm chores for girls. As you might guess, many never received the promised money and clothing.

Old newspapers provide some sad accounts of tragic incidents involving kids who were placed out. In 1932, a farmer in Blue Earth County, Lyle Waddell, was convicted in a Mankato court of poisoning 17-year-old Floyd Williams in order to collect a $3000 life insurance settlement on a policy he had taken out on the boy. The prosecutor argued that Floyd's period of service was nearly up, and that Waddell had poisoned the boy. Waddell claimed that Floyd had committed suicide. A jury found the man guilty, and he was sentenced to Stillwater State Prison. A series of appeals went all the way to the State Supreme Court, which unanimously upheld the conviction. Four years later, however, a state pardon board, whose members included Governor Hjalmer Petersen, pardoned Waddell. The pardon was denounced by the Mankato attorney who prosecuted the case and by others, but Waddell was a free man.

Unfortunately I've heard firsthand many, many sad stories of children who suffered cruel and humiliating treatment. Gene, for example, was made to live in the barn. Girls have told me they had to eat in the kitchen while the family ate in the dining room. "Remember, you're an orphan," was a frequent reminder. Beatings were common. Most were told they had to forget they ever had another family. "You live here now." If a child spoke up, as Vi did, she was promptly told, "You do as I say or you'll go back to the State School."

In his book *While the Locust Slept*, Peter Razor writes about his placement with a Caledonia farmer who started out sulky and eventually became violent. The man forced the boy to do most of the farm work, berated him, isolated him, and tried to make him quit school. When he was 17, Peter escaped after a severe beating and found a more suitable family when authorities became involved.

Joane was 8 years old when she was placed with a family. The first thing her new parents did was change her name. Losing this personal tie to her former life, her name, absolutely crushed her, but she had no say in the matter. This happened frequently. Some children were told they were adopted only to discover as adults that the legal process had never been completed. Although these acts or omissions may not strictly qualify as abusive or neglectful, they produced additional long-term problems for kids who had already suffered a major setback by being in the orphanage in the first place.

Many did return to the school by running away, or they were sent back because the family couldn't cope with an extra person at their house. Some were removed from their indenture situation when a child had the courage to tell the agent what was happening. Occasionally the agent showed up for a surprise visit and removed a child based on what he saw.

The agent had the power to return any child to the school, but often the family and the child put up a good front when the agent visited each year. Some children, afraid they wouldn't be believed, endured their suffering, believing their lives could be no better. Some girls were sexually abused by the father and/or sons in homes where they had been placed. Who would believe a State School girl over a respected family member?

Adoption and indenture created a double whammy for children who came to the school with siblings. First it meant the trauma of moving in with a new family. Second, it meant they probably would never see their siblings again, particularly if one was adopted.

Frances wrote me the following about her humiliating indenture experience and the loss of her siblings: "I don't want sympathy. I don't hate anyone and certainly do not want revenge. They say 'Forgive and Forget.' I truly forgive. The passage of time has allowed that. But how can I ease the pain? Would that were possible. Sorrow is grieving. I will forever grieve a lost childhood spent without my brothers. It's a terrible thing to separate siblings."

Little changed in the placement and supervision of children until the mid '30s, when members of the old guard passed away or retired and were replaced by younger administrators with new social ideas. For example, in the 1937 Biennial Report, Robert Mosher, Case Supervisor (formerly called "State Agent") complimented the board of controls for their initiative in breaking away from tradition and established order where older methods appeared unsatisfactory.

The first step, he stated, was their abandonment of the ancient, inflexible and much abused Indenture Contract. He went on to say he appreciated the added caseworkers who could better design an individual plan for the individual child. He recommended that poverty alone should no longer constitute sufficient cause for breaking up a home.

As for the permanent placement of children in homes, he explained the better options that were now available:

1. Adoption only for babies and small children
2. Free homes with no contractual agreement with foster families
3. Wage homes for children over 16 years of age who could be fitted into a semi-self-supporting status
4. Limited boarding home program, which was an option reserved for placement of Negro children and other children for whom adoption, free or wage home placement does not offer a plan that will suit the child's needs.

Other critical priorities Mosher asked for were:

1. Vocational training "It is clearly fallacious to assume that all older boys should be farmers and all older girls housemaids."
2. Psychological and psychiatric help for the children
3. Additional staff and facilities for preschool children "So more individual care and attention can be given them for better mental development."

While it was never the intent of the school to keep a child for years, it happened in many instances and for many reasons. Unfortunately, those children who spent several years at the school became institutionalized, which left them with certain deficiencies after they entered the real world.

Here are a few other bits of history. Besides the babies who were brought to the nursery by public officials, on occasion a newborn baby would be left on the grounds, where it was sure to be found. The nurses named these babies. Among them were Napoleon Bonaparte, Ulysses S. Grant and Florence Nightingale.

I told this story to a service club in Waseca a few years ago. Afterwards a lady in the crowd came up to me and said, "I'm Napoleon Bonaparte's daughter!" She found my talk very interesting, as Napoleon would never talk of the school with his family (which is very common with State Schoolers). His picture appears in the 1900 biannual report. He lived in Medford and died just a few years ago.

When Ulysses S. Grant was attending Owatonna High School, a teacher went to Principal F. Keen Young and said, "I can't call that kid Ulysses S. Grant!" Young merely said, "Sorry, that's his name."

In a talk I gave at the Morton Historical Society Annual Meeting, I was telling how occasionally a girl would get pregnant at the school. She would then be sent to the Sauk Centre State Home School for Girls. When the baby was born, it would be taken from her and brought back to our nursery, at which point it became a second generation Ward of the State.

The girls who worked in our nursery called them "Sauk Centre babies." The mother would have to stay in Sauk Centre after the baby was born because she was still a Ward of the State, and staying up there would ensure that she would not be seeing the guy who got her pregnant, who would still be in Owatonna. Not all "Sauk Centre babies" had mothers who came from our State School because girls from all over Minnesota were sent to Sauk Centre after they were labeled, "wayward," for one reason or another.

After my speech a woman came up to me and said, "I'm one of those babies." She went on to tell me that after 38 years she found her mother. They had only two years together before her mother died, but they were so happy to be reunited.

A Boy From C-11

My Turn Comes

Being placed out was always my fear. I was so young when I arrived at the State School that it was all I knew. The State School was my home, and I wanted to always stay there. Why not? I was comfortable in my cocoon, and I felt I belonged there.

My records show that in 1937 when I was 10 years old, the State Agent found a home for me a few miles north in Faribault. I was all set to go. I had already given away all my precious marbles, jacks and other small valuables. My brother Oscar later told me that when they told him I was to leave, it was the saddest day of his life. He had already lost the rest of his family, and now he would lose his last brother.

But before they could send me out, I had to have a physical examination. They found a hernia; in my records they wrote, "rupture," so all plans changed. I couldn't go to Faribault, and I was happy and relieved to be staying at the State School.

But bad news followed. My records indicate that I went through a series of injections in the "rupture" area that "produced excruciating pain for ten minutes at the site of the injection and extending to back." After the shots I was unable to walk, and they gave me "codeine for pain." At the conclusion of the series of injections, I had to wear a truss, which I presume was to keep the rupture from returning. A few years ago I asked my doctor if he ever heard of such a treatment, and he shook his head and said he'd never heard of it. My records state that in 1942 "hernia okay." Whatever it was, I guess it went away, but I will never forget that experience.

Oscar was eventually placed out to a home in St. Paul, a sad day for both of us. As my childhood years passed, the day I dreaded came, as I knew it would. I had just turned 16, and now I had to leave my home, my friends, and everything I knew and loved. The State Agent found a home for me in St. Paul. My records state: "Case #9164. Harvey Ronglien, c/o Mr. and Mrs. R. F. Burlingame, 409 East Page Street, St. Paul, Minnesota."

That fateful day was June 14, 1943. The morning sun was peeking into Cottage 3's windows, an introduction to a beautiful summer day. After eleven years, this was to be my last day at the Owatonna State Public School.

My exterior that day portrayed a teenager ready for anything the outside world could throw at him. My interior contained a scared little boy who wanted to cry, but couldn't. I had just turned 16, and big boys don't cry.

I bravely entered the State Agent's car that was to deliver me to 409 East Page in St. Paul. I was being placed in a "work home," and my life was about to change forever.

Since they were prepared and ready for my arrival, Mr. and Mrs. Burlingame greeted me warmly and seemed happy to accept me into their home. I cried myself to sleep that night at the beginning of the summer of 1943.

Although many State School kids longed to be placed in homes, I never did. Now I was part of a family, but I didn't fit. We came from two different worlds. I not only lacked communication skills, I simply didn't fit into a home environment. Although they did everything they could to please me, I was on edge all the time and felt I was walking on glass. I had grown up with thirty kids to a cottage, roughhousing in a building built for durability. I just couldn't adjust to living in a family environment.

Meal times were especially difficult. I was afraid of using their fine china, of soiling their bed linens. Worst of all, I had never had a conversation with an adult except to say, "Yes, Ma'am" or "No, Ma'am." I didn't know how to make small talk. In their decency, the Burlingames tried to ask me questions and draw me out of my shell. I hated it! I'd think, "Just leave me alone!"

In addition to my fear and discomfort, I felt lonely. I often cried in bed, even if I was 16 years old. I had come from a family of five hundred, and now I was an only child. I felt like they were smothering me, and I couldn't breathe. I kept thinking, "Just let me go back to the State School."

The Burlingames were janitorial and laundry supervisors at Miller Hospital, and they had to leave for work early. I had to start work later, and getting to work presented a challenge. I was supposed to catch a streetcar on the corner and then transfer to other streetcars three times. For a kid who was brought up in a self-contained village of 300 acres, this was really difficult.

My work at Miller Hospital presented even more challenges. Although my records state that I would work as a janitor, the job actually involved working in the laundry and running an elevator. With all men off to fight World War II, elderly women staffed the laundry. I didn't know how to communicate with them either, the place was hot, and I was miserable.

I had never even ridden in an elevator, so running one was tricky. The elevator would jerk and stop a few inches below or above the door opening. I was continually jerking the process, and people had to either step up or step down, and I felt inept.

The stress and heat made me perspire. One day the phone rang before I started out for work. Answering the phone, a new experience, I heard Mrs. Burlingame on the line. She said, "I don't want to embarrass you, but a few of the ladies complained of your body odor." She had a solution for me. She instructed me to go into her bedroom and find a bottle labeled "deodorant." She explained that this stuff would take care of my problem, and specified that I was to take it and rub it under my bare armpits. She said that from now on, I should use deodorant after every bath. This was my first and last lesson on B.O.

After work, my choice was to walk home, and it was a time of solace. I loved being alone with my thoughts after spending the day with people I couldn't communicate with. I was a 16-year-old boy with the communication skills of a 10-year-old. I was uncomfortable outside the State School, especially when dealing with adults.

My walk home was always interesting. I would walk the downtown streets, where the buildings and people intrigued me. What a difference there was between this and the little world from which I had come.

St. Paul bars, with their doors flung open in the summer heat, were a constant source of interest. I would glance in quickly, but could never see much. I could hear jukeboxes and the loud talk and laughter, and these things raised my curiosity.

I loved the smell of stale booze that drifted out to the sidewalk, and made up my mind that someday I would have to investigate to solve the mystery of what went on in those places.

After about two weeks of living in St. Paul, I hopped on a bus and returned to Owatonna to visit the people at the State School. I borrowed a pair of my brother's best pants, two sizes too big, but I wanted to show off to the kids and employees that I had made it big in the city. Little did they know, as I walked around the grounds acting superior, how much I missed them and yearned to be back. I probably didn't fool anyone. I cried myself to sleep again that night because I no longer belonged. I was an outsider, a memory.

Although I felt sad and displaced, there were some bright spots during that summer. I was transferred to the custodial department, so I didn't have to deal with old ladies and elevators. One afternoon when I was walking home I passed a pool hall that, interestingly, housed a gym in the basement where professional and amateur boxers trained. It was called Gibbon's Gym, and one afternoon I mustered enough nerve to go in.

The whole place seduced me and connected me with one of my fondest State School memories, the Golden Gloves program. I loved the sweaty, musty odor, the ring, the snorting of the boxers sparring, the punching bags, and the pictures and posters that covered the wall. I stood there like a virgin in a house of prostitution--16 years old and looking more like 12.

A man with a big hat and a bigger cigar yelled, "Wha da ya want kid?"

I stammered, "I've done a little fighting and was wondering....."

"Come on. Let's lace a pair of gloves on you, and we'll put you in the ring."

I must have looked pretty good because he asked me to come back the next day. I later learned that his name was Billy Colbert, and he ran the place.

Soon I was a member of the St. Paul Boxing team as their 135-pounder. This was at the height of World War II, and we would go to Ft. Snelling and box Army teams every Friday night to entertain the troops. Winners got $5, and losers got $3, but the money wasn't important to me. I was wanted, I belonged to a group, we pulled for each other, and Colbert liked me.

It was hard to win a decision because the judges were soldiers, and they favored their guys. One night I knew I had won, but the judges gave the soldier the decision. As the decision was announced, the crowd booed loudly. I thought they were booing me because they thought I hadn't put on a good enough fight. To my greatest surprise, as I walked down the steps of the ring and into the aisle leading to the dressing room, the soldiers started patting me on the back and yelling, "You won that fight, kid!" "Nice job!" It was one of the biggest thrills of my lifetime because every soldier was a hero to me.

Another night we put on a fight card at the St. Paul Armory for some kind of convention, and the crowd was involved in plenty of beer drinking, smoking and yelling. After my fight, I asked for a beer. Someone replied that I was too young, but then they relented. "Okay, as long as you were on the card." I took a swig, and it all came up through my nose. That was my first beer, but far from my last.

My brother Oscar also lived in St. Paul. One night we went to a street carnival, and a couple of older girls took an interest in us. After a time, my older and wiser brother strolled off into a dark, wooded area. Quickly my fair lady looked into my confused face at an inexperienced, naive boy. I knew what we both wanted, but my shy awkwardness protected my purity.

Another evening five of us former State Schoolers entered the Prom Ballroom. A certain group of guys who didn't take a fancy to our presence rudely invited us out to the parking lot to test our pugilistic skills. I guess we were invading their turf. Although they had mayhem on their minds, we soon unceremoniously deposited them on the parking lot. They may have known the neighborhood, but with our boxing background, we more than held our own.

As summer neared an end, I wanted to return to Owatonna to attend high school among people I knew rather than starting out new at Humboldt High School in St. Paul. I felt more secure in Owatonna. So unsettled, untamed, and unhappy, I chose happiness over pride. Without warning one bright morning I packed all my earthly belongings into a cardboard suitcase and caught a bus for Owatonna, my childhood home. As I look back today, I realize I didn't know how to receive or give love. The Burlingames were nice people who deserved an explanation for my exit, but I chose to split without discussing things with them, which was very unfair.

Slowly but surely, during World War II the State Public School had been closing its doors. Many items like sheets and machinery had been rationed during the war, and paper was in short supply. Worn out items had not been replaced. Our bed sheets were mended and re-mended. Boys who were of age left to join the Army or Navy. Younger boys were placed out on farms because most men were in the service. Likewise the girls were placed out in homes to work as maids because the women who had earned their living as maids before the war were leaving to work in factories--replacing men who went to fight the war.

Returning to the State School in 1943 was not an option for me or any other 16-year-old boy. The State School and the scope of its operations were winding down prior to its closure in 1945. Dire situations that had prevented people from keeping children among family members improved with the initiation of New Deal welfare programs. The national economy improved after the start of World War II, and educators and social agencies decided that children were better served by immediate placement in foster homes. Although I returned to the school for occasional visits with Miss Keefe, to participate in boxing, and to eat a couple of Thanksgiving dinners, the place was closing, and I was forced to move out into the real world.

When I arrived in Owatonna, I walked the streets not knowing where to go or what to do. Elwood Mahlman, who knew me from Golden Gloves boxing, drove by in his Enterprise Cleaning truck. He stopped and asked what I was doing, and I told him I was looking for a place to live. He suggested a few places, and eventually I ended up at Maude Johnson's room and board home at the corner of Rose and Elm.

I was happy to be back on familiar turf. I was back in Owatonna and living with five other State Schoolers plus three older men. With many men off to war, the King Company readily hired me. Since I was still a Ward of the State, my social worker checked on me but provided little, if any financial help. I was basically on my own.

Living at Maude's was an adventure in itself. Maude was a wonderful person and a great cook. Mr. Patterson, one of the men, was from New Jersey. He had packed up all his belongings and moved to Minnesota on the word of a fortune teller who had told him there was gold on a farm near Ellendale, fifteen miles from Owatonna. He had been digging the mine shaft for years, and until the day he died he believed that fortune teller. He was an entertaining guy who loved to sing and play the piano. Unfortunately he never found gold.

Maude was a Christian Scientist who didn't believe in doctors. She got a sore on her foot that got infected. It eventually forced her to stay in bed, and the infection got so bad that the odor permeated the entire house.

We couldn't take it, and the social service people finally forced her to go to the hospital, where they amputated her leg. She was a wonderful person who came to a tragic end, and every time I go by that house on Rose and Elm Street, I remember her and think of those days.

Forced to find new housing, State Schooler Bob Raymond and I found another board and room home with an elderly couple on South Cedar. We didn't have either a watch or a clock so we were forced to listen to our inner clocks. One morning we woke with a start thinking we were late for work. We quickly dressed and raced out the door. As we passed the courthouse, we noticed that the clock read 4:30 a.m. Our inner clocks were definitely off that day.

High School--Not a Priority

Summer passed, and I enrolled at Owatonna High School and continued to work half days. Although I wanted to return to Owatonna for high school, education was not my priority. I had no educational goals, and I went to school simply because I had to. My grades were poor, and I had too many other things on my mind. I was living on my own, and I knew I had to work to survive. The following excerpt is taken from a report filed by my social worker December 6, 1943.

"I talked to Harvey at school. We had previously heard that Harvey was having difficulty making his board and room payments. I stopped to determine what plans he had made for completing his payments. He stated he was still working at the Protecto Company earning $6 a week. Since his board and room amounted to $7 a week, he was running short. In November he owed $3.50. He was not particularly concerned about this since he stated he would be able to make this up during the Christmas holidays. He talked about his finances, how he was budgeting his money, what he was spending it for etc. It seems to me he has a pretty good money sense, as he is getting along very well. He stated that during the Christmas holidays he would be working full time and that his income would be considerably more."

After reading that, you can well imagine that money was tight. I had room and board to contend with, and although I was a Ward of the State until age 18, the State School never gave me a dime after I left the campus. I don't know how I made it because I also needed clothing and some money for entertainment. I worked full time in the summer so it worked out.

There probably weren't many Owatonna High School freshmen living on their own, but I was one of them. Although I had lived in the town for many years, I was unknown off the State School campus and shy in my new school environment. Being a healthy teenage boy, I wanted to spread my social wings and start dating. Even though I was unfamiliar with the skills or rules of courtship, I met a girl I wanted to take out. My first date was quite an exercise in futility, but one has to start somewhere.

She was one of the nicest people God ever put on this earth — well known, popular and a member of "the in group." Her name was Ethel Beaumont, and I liked her from the first day of high school. I think she felt the same about me, but since I had put her on a pedestal, I was a little intimidated by her.

Finally I mustered enough courage to ask Ethel if she would mind going to the movie with me. She graciously accepted my overture, and we agreed on the date and time.

Of course, I didn't have a car, but that was no problem because her house, my place, and the State Theater were all within walking distance. I was really treading on virgin ground in every sense of the word because I had never been on a date before, and had no clue about the protocol for this particular type of social situation.

I can't remember too much about the evening because it's been a long time. I vividly remember, however, arriving in front of her house, and when she wasn't outside waiting for me I was perplexed.

Hmmm…I thought that was strange so I walked around the block. When I came back to her house again, no Ethel. I stood out front on the sidewalk like a lost soul, wondering what to do now. It never dawned on me that maybe I should walk up to the door and knock.

Ethel had three older sisters. One of them probably looked out the window eventually and saw me standing out on the sidewalk and came to the justifiable conclusion that this dumb bunny didn't know enough to come to the door. After what seemed like an eternity, out came Ethel. With that roadblock removed, we were on our way to an evening of excitement and ecstasy. Well, not quite!

After the movie we walked to George's Café for a milkshake. Since my social skills were rudimentary, our conversation was forced, with frequent silent gaps. I'm sure we were both doing our best to impress one other, but it wasn't going all that well.

As we were walking from the café to Ethel's house, I was in turmoil about how to amorously end the evening. At her doorstep we looked at each other, then discreetly agreed that the evening had been an enchanting journey. A tender peck on the cheek ended our rendezvous.

My first date was history — but not quite. If my goal had been to have a relationship or score with the ladies, I fumbled at midfield and made a real mess of things. The next school day I was taking some heavy razzing from the guys about my love life. Instead of accepting the fact that I had just gone on my first date with a nice girl, I down played it and told the guys I took her out on a bet. I was like a child who thought liking a girl made you a sissy.

Even though she never confronted me, I could tell by her actions that my remarks got back to Ethel. She was embarrassed to think our date had been part of a dirty trick I played on her. She felt she had been made a fool of, and her feelings were hurt.

Ethel later married and moved to northern Minnesota, and I never saw her over the years. Sixty years later at an Owatonna High School class reunion, Ethel walked up to me and said, "Harvey, I've always wanted to ask you something."

I stopped her right there and explained that the story she heard about our first and only date had all been a lie. There had been no bet. Our date was legitimate. I just wasn't mature enough to admit I liked her, and I was still a boy from C-11 who thought preserving my tough-guy image with the guys was more important than any hurt feelings she might have suffered. After I explained how truly sorry I was for embarrassing her and confessed that my behavior had always bothered me too, we laughed and hugged. Finally my first date really was history.

As the months crawled by, I struggled through freshman year. My oldest sister Hazel, who always kept in touch with Oscar and me, moved with her husband to Bensonville, Illinois to work at a defense plant. She invited us to come there and live with them. We took the 400 train to Chicago, where my sister met us, and I got a job at Douglas Aircraft defense plant.

110

Working at Douglas Aircraft was exciting, and the pay was good. The plant was huge, covering acres. It was very intimidating to me, with thousands of employees under one roof and long rows of C-54 cargo planes. I rubbed shoulders with a lot of "Rosie the Riveters" because my job was to sort out the various sized rivets. It was a beautiful sight to see those large planes roll off the assembly line.

I didn't plan to return to Owatonna, but someone gave my ego a boost. The new Owatonna High School football coach, Paul Becker, wrote me a letter begging me to come back to play football. He had me mixed up with my brother Oscar, who had played the year before, but I didn't know that. His letter impressed me so much that I came back to Owatonna. Still thinking I was Oscar, Coach Becker put me at a starting position, and I played the season. I don't know if he ever did figure it out. To him I was just "Ronglien."

During that football season, a high school friend, J.D. Bringold, invited me to come up to his house after school. It sounded good to me so I accepted. When he arrived at his home he walked right in. I thought that was strange, to walk in without knocking. Then he yelled, "Hi Mom!" That shocked me! I had never heard that before and was shocked that a high school boy still called his mother "Mom."

I thought, "Gosh, J. D. is nothing but a big baby." That's how strange family life was for me. Today our adult children still call us Mom and Dad—it's as natural as can be. But that's how strange normal family interaction was for me after coming out of an institution.

Another shock about home life occurred that fall after the football season ended. Several parents hosted big meals in their homes for the football team. I remember going to the homes of Chuck Simon, Bob Neuleib and Dick Rakow. In addition to my amazement at seeing the huge variety of food, I was shocked when we went up to each boy's bedroom. Wow! To have your own bedroom with pictures and other paraphernalia—that really impressed me. I had no idea what life was like in a typical boy's home.

Another strange thing I started to notice was that people didn't always eat everything on their plates. This really surprised me. I had been brought up to believe that it was absolutely necessary to clean your plate before you left the table, whether you liked the food or not. No "ifs," "ands," or "buts." You ate it.

My sophomore year continued after football, with Golden Gloves during winter and baseball in the spring. Sports and work were my priorities. Since I lived in one room with nothing to do, I spent evenings at the movies or the pool hall (a place my social worker had warned me about). I believe I saw every movie shown at the State, Roxy and Tonna Theaters.

Jule Keefe, our last and most enlightened matron at the State School, let me come to her apartment sometimes in the evenings to listen to the radio, visit, and play cards. After my infancy, which I don't remember, she was the closest thing to a mother I ever experienced, and Oscar and I visited her until she died at age 92. We were her boys, and she loved us unconditionally.

As summer neared, my priority was getting into the Army. I was 14 on that infamous December 7 when I learned the news about the bombing of Pearl Harbor. I remember the older kids saying, "The Japs will be on their knees in two weeks."

I foolishly wanted the war to last because I wanted to see combat. I wanted to win the war and come home a hero. Didn't everybody in those days? In my youthful exuberance and naiveté, I thought war was glamorous, like in the movies.

Mr. Ostrander, our teacher, took a few minutes of his class to tell us of the Battle of Britain, along with the progress of the war. As time passed, the war became close and personal. First a kid from the State School was wounded in action, bayoneted on Guadalcanal.

Soon we learned another was captured at Bataan. Later still, another was killed in Bougainville. Then another was killed in the Coral Sea, on Tarawa, in North Africa, Italy, and the English Channel. On and on it went.

Writing of their deaths, the local newspaper reporters would proudly refer to them as "foster sons." They were one of us. They came from my extended and extensive family. I have no knowledge of the number of fatalities in other wars, but of those reported, World War II claimed twenty-four State School "sons."

In spite of the bad news, I wanted to be in the military. The minute I turned 17 in 1944, I went down to enlist in the Marines. To my surprise, I was turned down because of color blindness. "Okay," I thought, "I'll just go to the Navy recruiter."

I got the same answer. Broken hearted, I knew I'd have to wait until I was 18 before the Army would take me.

On May 5, 1945, my eighteenth birthday, I signed up for the draft and immediate induction, but I knew it would take a few weeks before they would call me up. Young and restless, with little to do, a childhood buddy, Bob Raymond, and I decided to do some hoboing. With no planning, no schedule, no destination, no money, no possessions, and no debts-- responsible only to ourselves, off we went. After walking the Rock Island tracks, we hopped a freight heading south. After ending up in Marshalltown, Iowa, we hopped another train and arrived in Albert Lea, Minnesota, north of Iowa and thirty miles from home. Poor navigating! Travel agents we weren't. In our quest to see the country, it was plain we were losing ground. So we hurriedly hopped another southbound train.

Next thing I remember, while we huddled under some cardboard, someone was shaking us and telling us, "This is the end of the line, boys." Tired, hungry and bruised, we trudged out to find a meal. Penniless, we decided to do some "back door bumming," chores for a meal. The elderly lady at the door studied us, as motley a pair as you're ever going to see. With a look of disgust, pity or whatever, she told us to stay put, and soon she returned with leftovers that tasted like a Roman feast.

With our bellies replenished and with renewed vigor, we got back on the chugging, groaning, smoke-belching iron horse headed for no place or any place. Because we got kicked off in the middle of nowhere for running on top of boxcars, we walked into Leavenworth, Kansas, and unlawfully confiscated a loaf of bread and quart of milk, which we eagerly devoured.

Catching a train out of Leavenworth, we made another major blunder and hopped on a gondola, one of those open, iron cars. By noon it was blazing hot, and we were like two eggs in a frying pan. As soon as the train slowed down, we jumped off in a frantic rush for water and shade. Believe me, riding the rails isn't for wimps.

While walking the tracks in Arkansas we stumbled onto a hobo jungle. Plentiful in the '30s, these places became rare in the '40s because of the job opportunities created by the war. When a hobo offered a bowl of soup, we inhaled it and then hung around and sat by the fire listening to stories. One hobo was playing the harmonica--downright elegant. Bedding down near the fire, we slept like babies. It was like we were adult Boy Scouts.

The next day, we hopped another freight and took another ride into the sunset. Not exactly among the elite of the hobos, we were grimy, filthy and hungry. We begged, stole, washed dishes, and mopped floors--anything to keep our midsections happy.

Finally, humbled and weary in Salinas, Kansas, we decided we'd had enough of trains. Hitchhiking had to be better. On our first try at thumbing, along came a police car. Lo and behold, I had left my draft card home, which at that time was a no-no. They threw me in jail. I had to prove that I was not dodging the draft, and it was Saturday, and my draft board was closed. They would have to hold me till Monday, but at least they served food. When my buddy came around to the barred window, we decided that he might as well head home without me.

To my surprise, a few hours later the police had a change of heart and let me out. With my thumb out, I hit the road. Darned if a few towns up the road, there was my buddy standing on the corner with his thumb waving. His mouth dropped when we drove up, and there was a smile on my face when we offered him a ride. Together again we were homeward bound. We limped into Owatonna older and wiser. We found there ain't no glamour on those mysterious tracks.

When we arrived home, my induction papers were in the mailbox. A few days later I was a member of the U. S. Army. Free meals, a bunk, and Uncle Sam paid for the travel. Hey, I never had it so good.

My Campaign in Italy

It was not my destiny to see combat. The war ended during my seventh week of basic training, but my time in Italy was an enlightening year, to say the least. For an 18-year-old boy who had spent his childhood on a postage stamp, seldom being off the grounds of an institution, the entire Army experience became a jolting lesson in life. Starting with basic training, I was metamorphosing into new growth. It opened me up like a butterfly when the wings have hardened and it's ready to fly away and begin its life in the air.

When we arrived at Camp Fannin in Texas, Sergeant Rickey assured us in a rather strong manner that we were the motliest God-awful recruits he had ever seen. He let us know how he doubted he could ever make soldiers out of us. After his tirade, he advised us to give our souls to God because our asses were his. Seventeen weeks later we left Camp Fannin, and Sergeant Rickey had to admit we were pretty darned good soldiers.

After seventeen weeks in Texas, I had a ten-day furlough before reporting for duty at Ft. Riley, Kansas. What should I do? I wanted to return to Owatonna, but I didn't have any place to stay and had little money to afford a hotel room. I can't remember how it came about, but Tom Bengtson, a friend from high school, invited me to stay at his home. His family was quite laid back, and his mom and dad accepted me with open arms.

Besides Tom, there was Jack, Dick, Don and Sammy. I don't think their little sister Susy had arrived yet. Heck, there's plenty of room! Come on aboard!

The first night I went out on the town, and when I came in, the little kids were sleeping on the living room floor. I tiptoed around them to the bedroom they assigned to me. For a minute I thought, "Gosh, I'm back in another orphanage." The entire family treated me great, and I'll always remember the kindness of the Bengtsons. The parents and Tom are gone now, but I treasure the memory of those people. They accepted me as one of the family. No questions asked.

When my furlough ended, I reported for duty in Italy. On the ship going over, the *USS Randolph*, I ran into fellow State Schooler Harvey Thomas, a Navy medic. It is always a coincidence encountering another person from that relatively small community, but it happens more often than you'd think. Penicillin had just been invented, and Harvey had been doing a brisk business giving shots to soldiers who had picked up various diseases in the States.

I became a man in Italy. Being there opened my eyes to the destruction of war and to the way other people live, and it showed me how little I knew about the outside world. There was life outside the State School and Owatonna. It taught me not to be so one-dimensional, to step outside the box, to live my life, be myself and enjoy the moment without being so rigid.

I saw the Coliseum in Rome and scaled the inside steps of the Tower of Pisa. I went up to Mount Casino, the bombed out monastery that caused such a stir during the war. On a clear day I could see the Isle of Capri. For months I lived in an encampment on the foothills of beautiful Mount Vesuvius. I saw awe-inspiring military cemeteries representing many different countries. I enjoyed my first winter without snow and marveled at the natural beauty of the countryside.

I sold cigarettes on the black market for $30 a carton. Rationed to a carton a week, we could buy a carton for a couple of bucks in the PX and sell them to the Italians. I learned women also enjoyed being seductive, contrary to my perceived notion that the man always had to be the initiator in the world of intimacy. Women taught me not to be so inhibited, that sex is universal and nothing to be ashamed of.

For a time I was assigned to guarding a German P.O.W. camp. Many of these prisoners had been a part of Rommel's famous Afrika Korps. If you think I didn't respect them, you're wrong.

The camp was fenced in and well guarded—or so we thought. The prisoners lived in large canvas tents. Somebody in command must have gotten the word that there was a little fraternizing going on, because one night we were ordered to check it out. Long after lights were out, we quietly surrounded the camp with trucks, then snapped on all the lights and stormed the premises. I never saw such a scampering of half-dressed female bodies running out of tents and crawling under the fence at well-placed crawl spaces.

My days were spent helping get rid of all the ammunition that was stored in big ammunition dumps around Naples. We supervised as Italians loaded the trucks, Germans drove the trucks to the docks, and then other Italian laborers loaded the ammo onto big, open rafts and took it out to the Mediterranean and dumped it overboard.

I had a good relationship with the German prisoners. I showed them respect, and they showed respect in return. Looking for outside news, they were always anxious to read my *Stars and Stripes*, a military newspaper. They were anxious to hear about the peace process and looked for news about when they would be allowed to go home.

After a few months I was shipped to the 88th Division, where we were more regimented. I was supposed to be there originally, but my orders got lost, enabling me to spend six months in the Naples area. I went north to Trieste on a troop train, and after we arrived we marched in orderly fashion to trucks that were to deliver us to our base. Oscar, meanwhile, on that very same day, was headed back south to get on the train that would take him to the ship that would take him back home. His outfit was headed one way while mine was headed the other way, and as we marched we were looking for each other. I just had a feeling that he might be there, and he had the same feeling about me. There were hundreds of soldiers in both groups, marching four abreast, and I don't remember who saw whom first and hollered out, but there we both were. All he said to me was, "Harvey—watch the women up here!" That's the advice he gave his little brother.

My training had been in the infantry, and the 88th was an infantry division. The Yugoslavians and Tito were presenting somewhat of a threat to the border in that region, so we were there to keep the peace. Although the war was over, occasionally a GI would die in some kind of scuffle or ambush so the soldiers in the 88th had to continue military training and drills like the ones they'd had in basic training.

Football was big in the military because it was a form of entertaining the troops. When there were football tryouts, there was a mad scramble for a position. If you made the football team, you were on "special service," which meant no more military training—just football.

On the day of the final cut, I couldn't make practice because I had to stand guard. I was lucky because even though I was not there for the cut, I made the squad by default. The coach let me hang on with the team. We had a special training diet and our own living quarters. Our top priorities were playing football, eating, and fraternizing with Italian women—not necessarily in that order. Life was good, and Italy unchained me from my childhood notions and set me free.

A Boy From C-11

Returning from the Military

I returned from Italy to Owatonna. Although I didn't like school, I wanted to get my diploma so I re-entered Owatonna High School. I also wanted to survive by working part-time. Sports and girls were also on my mind, and at times I'm not sure which held the highest priority. No wonder one of my report cards states, "Harvey has too many outside interests. School is not that important to him."

A lot of older guys finished high school after the war, and alongside the 16 and 17-year-olds, we felt like we were in a different league. I am grateful Owatonna High School permitted me to attend half days and condense my last two years into a year and a half, and I am also grateful to Owatonna Tool Company for giving me a part-time job. These considerations enabled me to graduate from Owatonna High School in 1948, after a year and a half of less-than-outstanding coursework.

I also owe my success to some personal strategies that worked well. During my first semester I was failing English. I really liked my teacher, Miss Lehman, and I went in and asked her to do me a favor. I showed her a scar in my eyebrow and said, "While you and all these kids were sitting home safely, I was overseas, fighting the war so you wouldn't lose your freedom." I told her that the scar was from shrapnel. Since it was close to my brain, the doctors couldn't remove it. I told her that I learned fast but couldn't retain, and she changed my F and gave me a passing grade. She didn't know I hadn't seen combat or, according to a story my sister Hazel told me, the scar was one I'd gotten when I fell out of the high chair as a baby.

Another time a teacher put a note on my desk and said she wanted to see me in her classroom after school. When I came in, her first words were, "You know, Harvey, I'm not much older than you." I'll leave the details to your imagination, but I passed her class too.

Of course, drinking and partying with my buddies was also a big part of my life now. One night after drinking, we stopped for gas at a local station. I got into an altercation with the attendant, and the cops were called. I unwisely fought the law and the law won. I was thrown into a cell for the night and released the next morning.

Just about the time I turned 21, I graduated. With my high school diploma in hand, I was faced with the dilemma of what to do next. I knew college was not for me, so I started thinking about going up north. I didn't have a car or know how to drive one, but fortunately I had friends with cars. One day Corky Johnson and I decided to head up north. I knew, through my sister, that I had a brother named Leonard in Nevis, but he was eight years older, and we had not seen each other since I was a tot. Corky said, "Let's look him up!" It turned out to be quite an experience.

After searching around, we found Leonard's little bar out in the woods, walked in, and sat down on a bar stool. I asked the bartender, "Aren't you going to serve your little brother a drink?" This was our first meeting, and while I wasn't affected much, Leonard became quite emotional and had to go off by himself for awhile. This was how I met my eldest brother.

When I returned from up north, I decided Owatonna was where I wanted to stay, and I was lucky to find a full-time job. I worked for a new company called Gopher Athletic, run by Jim Pofhal, Biff Barrett and Malcolm Stephenson. I was their first employee to be hired and their first to be fired. These fellows wanted to make me a salesman, selling athletic equipment to high schools and colleges. It took them less than a year to realize they had made a major mistake. I had several shortcomings as a salesman: I couldn't drive a car, my handwriting was pathetic, I was immature, and I was intimidated by anyone older than myself. As kindly as they could, they let me know I just wasn't qualified for the job. Today Gopher Sports employs ninety people and provides sporting goods and specialty items nation wide.

Before they let me go, as a young high school graduate, Army veteran, and working man in a small city in the late 1940s, I had it about as good as I had ever hoped to have it. So with a little change in my pocket, I was all set to conquer the world. Bob Reynolds, another State Schooler, was a friend of mine, and we had one adventure I will always remember.

Still somewhat flush with discharge money and free from the restrictions of military control, Bob and I felt invincible. One day my buddy, a carefree soul with an incomprehensible thought process, came to me with a problem. He had met the girl of his dreams, a Waseca girl who in his eyes was as beautiful as Betty Grable, the pin-up favorite of many GIs. He had asked her out for a date, and he needed my help.

He had a couple of minor roadblocks to overcome before said date. But since we were young and invincible, we did not consider these insurmountable. Bob saw himself as a suave, worldly man who was scheduled to knock on the young lady's door the next evening and escort her into a world she had never seen, in a style she was unaccustomed to. Up to this point, his plan seemed realistic for a guy of his age and status.

But the barriers suddenly came into focus. In rapid order, these problems included the fact that Bob didn't have a car, he didn't have a driver's license, and he had never driven a car. Waseca is about fifteen miles from Owatonna. He asked me if I would chauffeur him, but I didn't have a car either. I did not have a license, and I had never driven a car. Bob and I had grown up in the same place, a home where there was no father figure to take boys out and teach them to drive when we turned 15. We were a few years behind other young men our age, at least as far as driving was concerned.

The plan we concocted was ingenious. We would ignore the law. Who needed a license? We had just won the war; we could certainly buy a car. His pockets bulged with green. Everybody else was driving a car so it couldn't be that difficult.

Side by side we confidently marched into Mulken's Used Car Lot. After surveying the inventory and taking no test drive (we weren't much for details), we completed the transaction and proudly climbed into our vehicle of choice. Bob drove, and his plan was to deposit me at my place and then continue on with his evening's plans.

Of course, the car had standard transmission, and neither of us had any idea how to drive it. After grinding the gears severely, he wisely left it in one gear and maneuvered his way out of Mulken's to my little corner of the world. As he arrived at my residence, he mistakenly hit the gas pedal instead of the brake. Confusion reigned supreme as we lurched forward, jumped the curb and slammed into a sturdy oak.

Slightly flustered but uninjured and undaunted, we jumped from the car to measure the damages. Well, they were fairly extreme so adjustments had to be made. After further pondering our situation, we decided the car had to go. We limped back to Mulken's, and at a substantial loss to Bob's finances, they agreed to take the battered vehicle back. My friend had owned his first car for all of thirty minutes. As we left the car lot on foot, we looked back and saw Mulken's crew watching us with confused looks.

Bob thought he should notify the young lady about his transportation predicament, but upon questioning him, I discovered my pal didn't know Juliet's last name. How could we contact her? We could see no honorable way out. Consequently the seeds of a healthy relationship had been nipped in the bud before they could blossom into lasting love. Or maybe fate took over and rescued the fair maiden from a life of distress. We'll never know.

By springtime in 1949 I was playing on the Owatonna Aces baseball team. Jack Shimpach, one of the directors, learned I was unemployed and offered me a part-time job at the Owatonna Public Utilities. Knowing that I was living in one small room, he also offered me the opportunity to live in their home, where I could eat with his family. Since I had been eating all my meals in a restaurant, this sounded pretty good. However, my only previous experience living with a family had been with the Burlingames in St. Paul when I was 16 so I wondered how this would work out.

Jack was a real sports enthusiast, his daughter Jackie was involved in high school, and Louise was a good cook, so I felt comfortable. Maybe I didn't always live up to their expectations with my late hours, sleeping late on Sunday morning and other bad habits. I must say, however, that they were kind, gracious people whom I will always remember and appreciate.

By fall of 1949, I started working full-time at Owatonna Public Utilities, where I enjoyed a 35-year career. Starting as a grunt, I worked up to journeyman status, then first-class lineman. The job had its dangers, but it also gave me a sense of importance. Not everyone is up to the rigors of being a lineman, but for me the job was an excellent fit. I had the opportunity to work outdoors, and every day was different—climbing poles, digging holes, dealing with low voltage, high voltage, in sleet, rain, snow and mud.

Storms created emergency situations, and the customers who depended on us had to be served. It was a great occupation, and I loved the environment of working with a gang of guys in the outdoors. I loved and appreciated my job and the people I worked with, and I will always be grateful to the Owatonna Public Utilities for giving me such a great opportunity to support my family with a meaningful job that suited me so well.

I was 18, and shortly after a little send-off party with coffee and donuts, I posed for my official Army portrait.

In Italy a few months later, I looked like a real soldier.

Top left: Being chosen to play for an Army football team gave me some privileges and kept me out of drills.

Right: At age 21, I graduated from Owatonna High School.

Left: I became a lineman for Owatonna Municipal Utilities, a job I liked and for which I was well suited.

A Lifesaving Door Opens

Life was good. I was working as a grunt with the line crew at Owatonna Municipal Utilities and playing baseball with the Owatonna Aces and living with the Shimpach family. Some of my friends had cars for cruising, and I enjoyed hanging around the Valencia Café and pool hall.

One night a couple of us decided to drive out to the Monterey Ballroom to check out the action. We heard there was a wedding dance, but of course we didn't plan to dance. I had never danced in my life. Soon a bunch of high school girls whom we knew stopped by, but there was a new girl I had never seen before. Someone introduced her as Maxine Grunklee.

A few days later, on Saturday afternoon, I had just picked up my laundry when I noticed Maxine sitting in a car across the street. I walked over to say hi, and we had a little chat. She introduced me to her 10-year-old brother Dale in the back seat. I could see that Dale was mentally retarded, but this didn't faze me. However, Maxine was sure that would be the end of whatever relationship might have begun because mentally retarded people were shunned in 1949. That's probably why Maxine stayed in the car with Dale while her mother shopped.

A few days later, on Flag Day, I ran into Maxine and her friends at an evening parade. As we talked I learned that she was already driving a car. Here I was, a 23-year-old hotshot, and I couldn't drive. I connived to meet her again the next night if she could get the car, and we planned a special meeting place. Maxine was only 16, and I knew my buddies would razz me for

131

robbing the cradle. Maxine's friends had warned her to watch out, because Harvey was just a playboy. Nevertheless, we pulled off our secret rendezvous, and I was very impressed.

The very next day I thought, "I've got to get a car, but I don't even have a driver's license or know how to drive." Stupid me! I should have gotten a license years earlier when it cost 50 cents and no test was required.

Love and infatuation are great motivators, so I asked one of the guys at work how to go about carrying out my plan. He told me that I needed to get a license first, and suggested that I take one of the company trucks to take the test. I failed the test miserably.

Back to the drawing board I went. My friend said I could use his car, and he suggested he give me a few lessons first. I failed my second test even worse. This time the examiner said, "Stop the car!" And he got out and walked back to the courthouse.

Now what? I made it back to the Utilities, safely returning the car. After more practice, I took the test a third time and became a licensed driver at the age of 23. Now I was ready to take my next big step--buying a car. What did I know about cars? I walked over to the downtown used car lot and thought that little 1946 coupe looked pretty good. I asked my buddies, "Now how do I get the money to pay for it?"

They looked at me like I was a dunce and said, "Go to the bank and ask for a loan to pay it off monthly." What a greenhorn I was! I had no clue how things were done because this is the sort of thing parents explain to their children. I knew nothing about business or money. All I knew was that if I didn't have cash in my pocket, I didn't buy anything.

I shyly went to the bank and said, "I need $640 to buy a car." Gosh, they were nice to me. Since I was working, they would gladly loan me the money. Now I had a car. Maybe I still wasn't the best driver in the world, but Maxine patiently helped me learn the fine points.

Maxine was a very mature 16-year-old who had grown up on a farm southeast of Owatonna, where she learned responsibility at an early age. She came from a very good Christian family that cherished family and their faith. So age never was a factor in our relationship. We discovered later, however, that I brought a lot of baggage into our relationship from my childhood, baggage that would be difficult to deal with.

I had a car, but since we had to continue to keep our courtship secret, our favorite date was simply driving to a remote spot where we could talk and spoon. Maxine loved hearing me tell tales from my childhood, about being in the Army, the Golden Gloves and my many antics.

I started to hear about her early life, family and church. This was a whole new world for me. While her parents questioned our age difference, they liked me, and Dale would sit by the window waiting for me to come and pick up Maxine.

When I was invited into their home, Dale and I struck up an instant relationship. He loved to be teased, and he loved the attention I gave him. Dale gave me some of my happiest moments, and I am sure I returned the favor.

My relationship with Maxine continued to bloom as this little farm girl wormed her way into my heart. I felt I was standing in quicksand. The more we saw of each other, the deeper my feelings grew. As our relationship progressed, it got to where neither of us would break it off. We had spun a web neither of us could or wanted to free ourselves from. We couldn't get enough of each other. Maybe this was meant to be, so why hide it? We finally went public.

We had some pretty rocky times because of my wandering ways. Several times Maxine called off the courtship. In fact, this happened two months before our planned wedding. One evening I told her I was going to a union meeting, but I strayed off course and ended up with a girl at a 3.2 beer joint in Bixby. As fate would have it, Maxine and her mother, on their way to her aunt's house fire, drove by the beer joint and saw my car. To my amazement, Maxine walked in, slapped her engagement ring down on the pinball machine that my date and I were playing, and walked out the door.

The next day Maxine called me and told me to come and pick up every trinket I had ever given her. Her mother backed her a hundred percent, saying, "You're going off to nurses' training."

Well, we eventually overcame that obstacle, and we were married on December 27, 1952, in the country church where Maxine had been baptized and confirmed. Special guests included my dad, Eddie Rognlin, and my sister Hazel and her family. Other than one visit to the State School, this was the only time my dad ever came to see me.

Because family was important to Maxine, she planned our wedding rather quickly. Maxine's brother Norman, who was serving in the Air Force, was home on furlough before leaving for Korea, and she wanted him to attend our wedding. Since we didn't have much money, we spent our honeymoon at the Curtis Hotel in Minneapolis.

I was 25 by then, a full-time journeyman lineman, and Maxine worked at Federated Insurance. We lived in an apartment above her parents, and Dale spent as much time upstairs with us as downstairs with his mom and dad. Two years later we were blessed with our son Rob, and Maxine had to quit her job to become a full-time mother.

Since we wanted to have two children close together, Maxine again became pregnant in late 1954. The next spring we were attending Wednesday evening Lenten service, and suddenly Maxine leaned over to me and said, "Something is terribly wrong with me." As she stood up, blood came rushing down her legs. I scooped her up and carried her to a room near the entrance of the church. After laying her on the floor, I hurried out and drove the car up to the entrance of the church. I took her to the hospital, where she was put on bed rest for a week. Unable to hold back delivery, Maxine gave birth to our second son three months prematurely. I knew there was trouble when I heard Dr. Roberts order the nurse to "baptize this baby immediately." Weighing less than two pounds and with other visible problems, our second son died thirteen hours later. With Maxine unable to leave the hospital, her mother Leora assisted me in arranging for a small funeral and burial. This was my first experience in dealing with a family death.

Hoping for still another child, Maxine became pregnant for a third time, and her due date was May 18, 1956. While we were looking forward to this joyful event, we were jolted with two more unexpected deaths in mid-May. First, Maxine's father Herman suffered a major stroke. He was a kind, Christian man, and I took my turn staying with him at the hospital.

One morning I arrived home at 6 a.m. and was startled to learn that Maxine had just spoken to my sister Hazel on the phone. She informed me that my father Eddie had died that night from a fall down some basement stairs. The next day I was on my way to help Hazel with my dad's funeral arrangements, and coincidentally, Maxine's father died that same day. By the time I got back to Owatonna, the funeral for Herman had been held on May 18, the day our baby was due. Not only did our fathers pass away on almost the same day, they were both 63 years old. Other than that, they had very little in common.

I had definitely learned to deal with family deaths in a very short period of time, but our grief was replaced by joy a couple of weeks later when our little daughter Cheryl was born on June 4, 1956. Our family was now complete with a boy and a girl.

Some months after Maxine's father passed away, her mother offered to baby-sit our children so Maxine could return to Federated. Our small apartment was getting cramped, and

Maxine started to suggest we get our own home. Wow! I never dreamed all this would be happening, but I understood the need. Maxine, of course, had to handle all the details for this giant undertaking. When it came to a mortgage, homeowner's insurance, a checking account and paying bills, I was lost. I was used to people taking care of me so I left the responsibility for all these matters to Maxine.

Frankly, I had never envisioned myself getting married, having children, or owning a home. I realize that at every plateau in life, Maxine has had to take me by the hand and lead me to the next level. She likes to razz me that had I married some floozy, I'd be on skid row today. And you know, I think she's right.

By the time our children were born and Maxine was back at work, Dale was 13 years old, and Maxine's mother felt the best place for him would be at Bethesda Lutheran Home in Watertown, Wisconsin. Maxine and I argued that we would always care for Dale, but Maxine's mother wisely said, "No, you have children of your own to raise. At Bethesda Dale can learn more about the Lord, and maybe he can be trained in a trade."

She, of course, was right, but driving Dale to Bethesda and leaving him there was one of the most gut-wrenching experiences of our lives. We brought him home every summer for a two-week stay, but it was always heart breaking to take him back. Dale was a very special person in our lives.

While my humor often kept happiness in our home, there were many difficult times. My image is a happy-go-lucky guy without a worry in the world. Underneath this facade rages anger that has to be controlled. The class clown is unhappy inside.

Our diverse backgrounds were beginning to affect our marriage as Maxine struggled to teach me about family values and relationships. Family functions were foreign to me, and it was hard to see why they were so important. Having fun in bars, partying and sports were right up my alley. Somehow we worked our way through many trials. Each new phase of our children's lives and our extended families' lives became a first-time experience for me with baptisms, school, Sunday school, confirmations, graduations, weddings and funerals.

Church was very important to Maxine, and she wanted church attendance to be part of our children's upbringing. I preferred sleeping on Sunday morning and would argue that the Bible contained fairy tales. Remember, I vowed at the State School that I would never, ever go to church again, but Maxine hung in there.

Maxine had to handle disciplining the children, dealing with family problems, and all money matters. My selfishness kept me from being a really good parent, but I was a good provider. In addition to my full-time job at Owatonna Utilities, I worked many part-time jobs in the evenings and on Saturdays.

I certainly wasn't going to abuse my children like I had been abused. My greatest joy was spending time with the kids shooting baskets, playing catch or getting a neighborhood ball game going. A couple of parents thought I was one of the kids because their children would hurry to eat so they could get out "to play ball with Harvey."

I was good at having fun with the kids, but when it came to counseling them, encouraging their education, and role modeling, I guess I fell short. Coming home intoxicated wasn't good role modeling, nor was coming to the breakfast table with a hand broken in a fight the night before. I was definitely giving our children a lot of confusing messages--don't do these things that I do. I'll always be grateful for Maxine's common sense, her Christian values, and her ability to serve as the anchor of the family. I'm also proud to say that in spite of my shortcomings, both our children graduated from Minnesota State University at Mankato.

Soon after our son graduated from college, we gained a daughter-in-law, Deb, and then our granddaughter Tiffany. With the children gone, we became empty nesters. Our social life revolved around drinking. Weekends found us at local clubs or with friends who enjoyed partying like I did. Maxine complained about my drinking and behavior, and I always promised that things would change. But what would we do if we didn't drink and party? While Maxine drank responsibly, she didn't realize at the time that she was acting as my chief enabler.

Sports were my big interest, and I managed the Eagles softball team, and in 1975 we took the national championship. I also coached a boxing team in the late 1970s, and there were many rewards working with those young people. But I also enjoyed the drinking and partying that went with it.

I was involved in an early morning car accident in front of St. Joseph's Church, where I totaled out two cars, including my own. The crash woke the priest, who called the ambulance.

I ended up in the hospital, and ironically, the parked car I had totaled belonged to the head nurse on duty that night in the hospital.

The priest called Maxine at 1 a.m. to inform her of the accident. After rushing to the hospital, Maxine found a drunken husband pleading to go home. "I really screwed up this time." Since I felt no pain, they released me, but the next morning I begged to return to the hospital. After the alcohol wore off, the severe pain of broken ribs set in. I spent two days in the hospital, vowing I'd had my last drink. Not realizing the strength of the addiction, I soon returned to my old ways. However, Maxine gave me rides uptown. At least I wouldn't kill myself or others driving home.

One Labor Day, a friend and I headed up to Hoff's Bar for "a beer." A few hours later I got into it with a guy, and the brawl continued out on the street. After the police broke it up, I headed across the street to the American Legion for—you guessed it—another beer.

It wasn't long before the police came into the Legion and informed me that my opponent's wife was pressing charges. I was booked at the jail, but they let me go when Maxine picked me up and took me home.

But that's not the end of the story. To my amazement, the doorbell rang on the afternoon of the following Christmas Eve. When I opened the door I saw the two police officers who had booked me on Labor Day, and they presented me with a bottle of Seagrams whiskey.

Their comment was, "For services rendered on Labor Day." They had previously incurred many problems with my Labor Day opponent, and they were happy he had gotten his comeuppance. That was a strange Christmas present, and it was ironic that the police who took me to jail when I was drunk in September gave me a bottle of whiskey three months later.

After another night on the town, I woke up with a broken hand, the result of a slight altercation with another drinker. I hadn't learned my lesson, and old John Barleycorn had led me astray again. Old John always had the magical powers to make me think I wasn't only the world's greatest lover, but also the heavyweight champion of the world.

My pugilistic skill betrayed me another night, and I awoke the next morning with a broken jaw. Other than my family, not another soul knew about this incident. I never missed work, kept my mouth shut, and lived sipping through a straw and eating very soft foods that didn't require chewing.

Several weeks later I went to my dentist, Dr. Ron Baker, because of a cracked wisdom tooth. When I opened my mouth he gasped, "Harvey, you've got a broken jaw." He advised me to wait a few more weeks for the jaw to heal before pulling the tooth. Dr. Baker has passed away, and my dental records are now in the hands of Dr. Jeff Huxford. He confirms that I had a fractured left jaw in 1971.

Streaking was a big fad in the 1970s. I had to be the class clown and streak through a Pizza Hut. Even as a mature adult I'd do anything for attention...all the result of the insanity of alcoholism and, no doubt, lack of attention in my childhood. In my alcoholic fog, I never thought of the embarrassment endured by my family. Unbeknownst to me, our son Rob had a life-changing experience in store for me.

On December 27, 1952, Maxine and I were married in the little country church where she had been baptized.

Top: A quarter century after we posed on the courthouse steps, my siblings and I again stood together after we buried a dad we barely knew.

Below: A few years later, my kids Rob and Cheri definitely had a hands-on dad, but I was not being a very good role model.

Entering Hazelden

Before my son could act on his plan, an important family transition occurred which, coincidentally, enabled him to proceed. We received a phone call that Dale had died from a heart condition at age 41. His funeral on Saturday presented a circumstance that would change our lives because it gave our children a perfectly timed opportunity to be home for the upcoming event planned for 7 a.m. Sunday morning.

For Maxine, the question of why the Lord had given her family a mentally retarded child was answered. To her, Dale's death signaled the oncoming rebirth of my life. I can't argue with her. Dale touched me deeply. I cried at his funeral that Saturday as I was reminded of his unconditional love for me. His death provided the time and place for the confrontation of my life.

Without realizing it, I was dramatically affecting my family by my drinking. On January 11, 1981, my son Rob, daughter Cheri and wife Maxine confronted me. My father and his father were alcoholics. Now my family, led by my son Rob, decided it was time to break the cycle. This family gathering was an INTERVENTION.

The proof was presented in a direct but loving manner. I had a problem, and it was time I faced it. After a heart-rending, tear-jerking few hours, I was on my way to the Hazelden Foundation at Center City for the treatment of alcoholism.

When word got back to Owatonna that I went to treatment, it surprised a lot of my fellow workers and friends. I can understand that because I rarely missed work. They would see my partying and carrying on as I had a good time. What they didn't see or know about were the crying jags, the blackouts, anger within and selfishness.

As we entered the grounds of Hazelden, I was amazed at the beautiful setting. The winding, wooded road led to an impressive set of buildings sitting on the shores of a lake frozen over and surrounded by woods. I was received cheerfully with dignity and kindness. Soon I was led to my unit to meet the "drunks and addicts" I would live with for thirty-two days. But as I was being introduced around, I wondered, "Where are they?" I was meeting clean, impressive, intelligent people, and among them were a college professor, a priest, a number of attorneys, a school administrator and a movie producer.

Contrary to common belief, ninety-five percent of alcoholics are not down and out. My roommate was a multimillionaire with a nationally known name you would all recognize. We came from all sections of the country. We weren't here for our appearance; we were here for our behavior. Our only common bond was our addiction and our desire to get rid of it.

I will always be grateful to the staff at Hazelden. They opened the door for me to really look into myself. What made me tick? What demons was I fighting? I was filled with anger and skepticism. I was harboring the effects of being abandoned in my early childhood; first my mother was gone, then my father.

146

Then one by one my siblings left, and then three homes that took me in rejected me. All of this happened before someone delivered me to institutional life that would last for eleven years.

The first day at Hazelden a counselor interviewed me. Her opening question was, "Did you experience anything traumatic during your childhood?"

I said, "No, not really, nothing that I can think of."

She kept hammering away until I finally said, "Well, I ran away a few times."

"Ran away from where?" She asked.

"The State School," I replied.

"The State School? What was that?" She asked.

"Kind of like an orphanage."

Her eyes widened like she had just struck gold. "Don't you think that was something traumatic? Going to an orphanage and losing your family?"

"Well, no," I answered. "I just figured that's the way it was. That was my life."

From that moment on, Hazelden took me on a thirty-two day journey that saved my life. I thank them for that. During group discussions we tore each other apart, but I grew to respect each of them. Between the tears, laughter, depression and encouragement, something positive was happening. Our attitudes were changing. We were heading in the right direction.

Slowly the conning ceased, replaced by sincerity, honest growth and serenity. It was a stimulating, interesting and enriching thirty-two days, a fantastic education and experience. Being forced to recognize one's character weaknesses is a humbling experience. I went through deflation, surrender, confession, restitution and giving. It works! I don't know why, but it works.

There is no problem so bad that booze doesn't make it worse. One excuse we offer is that we drink because we have problems. Fact is, we have problems because we drink. Or we drink to kill time, but we don't kill time. Time kills us.

Once you're an alcoholic, sobriety is an ongoing battle because you will always remain an alcoholic. A likely comparison would be--once a cucumber becomes a pickle, it can never be a cucumber again. Alcoholism has no restrictions as to wealth, color, education, age or position in the community.

A person who drinks excessively hurts most of the people he/she holds dearest--not intentionally, but it's the nature of the beast. Alcoholism makes for a dysfunctional family that will carry scars forever. That "life of the party" stuff is a charade. The other party goers aren't aware of the blackouts, and they don't see the depression or mental abuse of the alcoholic's family.

I've learned happiness isn't being the loudest at the party or always being where the action is. Happiness is deeper than that and more meaningful. Happiness is many things, a few of which are a good self image, being comfortable with yourself, and knowing that if you fail at something, it doesn't make you a failure as a person. Happiness is serene. It's coming to grips with a higher power. It's knowing that within us all lie enough good qualities that we don't need mood-altering drugs for added confidence. It's knowing you're not perfect and knowing you don't have to be. Happiness is knowing that to be loved you have to be lovable.

I challenged John Barleycorn, and it was a mismatch. It was a fight I couldn't win. He's relentless. He's filled our prisons and divorce courts, broken hearts and shattered dreams. Hey, once he gets the upper hand, he's one tough bird. If you fight him on his terms, you lose. It's that simple. Like my son told me at the intervention, "Dad, it will get you. One way or the other, IT WILL GET YOU!"

I finally wised up when I traded old John B. for my family, dignity and self-respect. It was the best deal I ever made. After my stay at Hazelden, I returned to work at the Owatonna Utilities as the night troubleshooter, taking all customer electric, gas and water calls. It was a rewarding experience. I took early retirement in 1984 and immediately took on a part-time job delivering car parts, a job I still enjoy. I thank the State School for teaching me a good work ethic.

Trading Booze for News

After Hazelden, my second home became the public library, one block from our home. I occasionally think back to the time at the State School when an angry matron yelled at me and asked why I didn't read a book once in awhile instead of fighting and roughhousing all the time. Of course, she wanted to control me, not educate me.

A few years later, another more understanding matron shared her newspaper with us boys, and she noticed how I only read the sports section. She tried to explain in a kind way that the editorial page was also interesting. She made that suggestion because she cared for me.

Unfortunately, neither woman affected any change in me. How could these two older ladies take it upon themselves to tell me how I should nourish my mind? Didn't they know I was almost shaving age? There wasn't a whole heck of a lot I didn't already know. Books and editorial pages were for bookworms, sissies and misfits.

It turns out that I learned a lot after I knew it all. Those two ladies are no longer with us, and if they were, they wouldn't believe what I'm going to say next. I not only read the editorial pages of several daily papers, I bury myself in world events as recorded by top news magazines. I'm never without a nonfiction book at home.

It's interesting how our priorities change. I used to treat bars with the same reverence. I'm not knocking bars, because I had a lot of fun in them. I enjoyed the banter, the companionship and the booze. I craved the atmosphere and attention. There were also a lot of highs and lows, but very little serenity. It wasn't the establishment's fault; it was my fault. I couldn't handle it. I finally didn't like what it was doing to my life, so you might say I traded booze for news. I just wonder if those two matrons may have known something many years ago. Do you suppose?

In 1988 the *Owatonna People's Press* invited local citizens to become board contributors for the paper. I took up the challenge and wrote many articles about life at the State School. My columns became a great tool in educating the community about the forgotten history of the State School. Writing has given me new self-confidence and a new lease on life. I love reading, research and learning. Educating myself has become a passion. It gives me serenity. My family kids me that it has become my new addiction, and that's good.

A New Life Begins

Going to Hazelden changed the course of our lives. Our marriage took on new meaning, and we began to enjoy the simple things in life that we had long overlooked. Walking together became a favorite pastime. Recovery brought new friends, new activities and new interests. Instead of partying, I was now attending weekly AA meetings, and Maxine was involved with Alanon. Spirituality took on new meaning when I realized I didn't need alcohol as a crutch.

Without realizing it, Maxine and I were acquiring new skills that would make us a good team in preserving the State School history. Maxine had developed excellent clerical skills as a private secretary. For me, Hazelden had opened up new channels to help me better understand how being institutionalized as a child gave me character flaws that I had to conquer. I also started to research and learn how the effects of being abandoned and having trust broken as a child can have lifelong effects.

By 1992, Maxine started to sense her company travel was affecting our marriage, and she remembered the abandonment I suffered as a child, which made it hard for me to be alone. Her decision was easy, and she chose me over her career and she took early retirement, thus ending her thirty-seven-year career with Federated Insurance.

After the orphanage closed in 1945, the campus functioned as a state institution that provided academic and vocational programs for educable adolescents who were mentally challenged. In most cases, their home communities provided no training beyond eighth grade, so this school provided a needed service. By the end of the 1960s, Title VI of the 1964 Civil Rights act and the Education of the Handicapped Act provided for significant federal funding for the education of all children age 3-21 within their home communities. Children who had been sent to Owatonna were now able to stay home and attend school and vocational training.

The State School campus with its cottages, classrooms, dining rooms and gyms that had housed, fed and educated children from the Victorian era to the Nixon years, closed its doors in 1970 and began to take on the look of abandoned buildings.

The original State School property had consisted of 160 acres. By 1937, there were 42 acres of campus buildings, paths, playground areas, athletic fields, and green space and 287 acres for agriculture. After 1970, the buildings and other property stood empty and unused for four years until the city of Owatonna purchased the campus in 1974 and renamed it West Hills. The cemetery had been all but forgotten in the community.

The thirteen original State School buildings today house city administration offices and other related city facilities, such as the Arts Center, Head Start and Seniorplace. The farmland became the city's industrial park, and a local realtor purchased the remaining property on State Avenue.

Cottages 4, 5 and 16 (the original school building) were demolished, and others were converted to apartment houses. The Owatonna Little Theatre and Wee Pals now occupy Merrill Hall, which housed our newly built school and auditorium when I first arrived.

By 1992, I had been lamenting the fact that in another generation or two, no one would remember that West Hills had been an orphanage for sixty years, nor would they remember the children who lived its history. Very little had been written about it, even many local people knew nothing of its history, and those of us who had been there right at the end were starting to get up in years. "If only there was a statue or something on the grounds that told its story," I kept saying.

Maxine finally said, "Well, Harvey, the only way it will happen is if we check into some possibilities." The rest, of course, is now history. We received the approval of the city council and funding from private donations. The erection of the "State School Kids" memorial began a new journey in our lives.

While we were fundraising for the "State School Kids Memorial" in late 1992, local citizen Bud Blekeberg came to us and said, "All those children in the cemetery should not be forgotten."

Bud asked if he could build a cemetery memorial. The cemetery, located in the southwest corner of the campus, is the final resting place for 198 children who were not claimed by family. The average age of those buried is 4 years old. Over the years, the cemetery had literally been forgotten behind a fence and locked gate, and few Owatonna residents even knew it existed.

Bud was given the city's approval to erect a memorial, and I was honored when he asked me to write the epitaph:

**TO THE CHILDREN WHO REST HERE
MAY THE LOVE YOU LACKED IN LIFE
NOW BE YOUR REWARD IN HEAVEN
YOU ARE REMEMBERED**

Bud's next proposal was to erect 151 crosses bearing the names of the children whose graves had been marked only by their numbers etched in a slab of cement. We again joined Bud for this effort, as did many volunteers in the community. A former employee, Ruth Gross, commented to me, "Sad, isn't it? These children who were deprived of a family in life were also deprived of their very name in death. But there is joy in heaven today because so many people cared." When completed, this project became an inspiration for friends and relatives who had loved ones buried by a number in other state institution cemeteries.

When I had earlier approached the city council for permission to erect a State School Kids Memorial, councilwoman Mary Jane Taylor asked us to consider starting a museum. Since the small turret room near the front door in the Main Building was not being used, we took up her idea and used that room to start a fledgling museum. All Maxine and I had were a few of my pictures, trophies Superintendent Henderson had given me when the place ceased to be a school in 1970, and a 1897 biannual book that contained a few pictures. But a small first museum had become a reality.

With the accomplishment of the State School Kids Memorial, cemetery restoration, and a small museum under our belts, we set out to plan a dedication ceremony to be held July 3, 1993. The community and former State Schoolers had graciously supported us, and many were planning to attend. I published the following article in the *Owatonna People's Press* that morning, summing up my feelings of accomplishment:

Today when the Orphan's Memorial is unveiled to the world, this heart of mine will humbly pound with pride. This, of course, is the culmination of a lot of work, generosity, and time from many people. It is with tremendous gratitude I acknowledge this.

In our childhood, our lives are in someone else's hands. We have no control. If we are fortunate, the owner of those hands will love and guide us. In my childhood, due to circumstances I couldn't control, I grew up at the State School. I made many lifelong friends there.

As I grew to an age when I could dictate the path I would travel, I walked some dusty roads, climbed a lot of hills, and crawled out of a lot of valleys. I crossed bridges and swam rivers. I've been up and I've been down. I've done a lot of things—some good, some bad.

Now, as the sand runs low in the hourglass of my life, I reflect on my life at the State School and the many friends I grew up with. Leaving this lasting memorial to honor all the State School children is my legacy to them, "The State School Kids."

I feel I've accomplished something. But I'm enough of a realist to know that without my wife Maxine and I, it never would have happened. In a few generations the State School would have been forgotten forever. This not only would have been a grave waste of a historic treasure, it also would have been a grave injustice to every former State School Ward. I couldn't be prouder than I am this day.

I was also very proud to give the keynote speech at the dedication ceremony, held in front of the Main Building. With more than 500 people in attendance, it was an exciting event. My comments follow:

Thank you and good morning!

I want to personally thank all of you who contributed in any way to make this day a reality. I also want to thank all of you who were interested enough to come here today. Serving as the spokesperson for the children of the Owatonna State School, I hope I'm intelligent and sensitive enough to do justice to this occasion.

We considered having Governor Carlson and other politicians speak today, but then we said, "Wait a minute. Administrators and politicians have spoken for us for 105 years. This institution was our home. They weren't here. We'll speak for ourselves today. This is the day of the 'State School kid.'"

The headline in the Owatonna paper on the morning of August 9, 1886 said, "The Heavens Smiled and the People Rejoiced." These headlines referred to a ceremony that took place earlier that week celebrating the laying of the cornerstone of the Owatonna State Public School, which, incidentally, was right in that corner.

We are here today, 105 years later, to make sure this institution and the children who made up its population do not fade from the archives of Owatonna's history--and from the history of Minnesota.

For those of you who aren't aware, this State Public School was a home for orphans and dependent and neglected children, created by an act of legislature in 1885. One of the first three children who entered this institution in December of 1886 was Alma Dennis. Ironically, Alma never left the school. She stayed on after age 18 and worked here until retirement.

The Owatonna State Public school survived for 60 years, from 1886 to 1945. In the hourglass of time, this was a brief moment. But it was a historic moment in this city's and this state's history because it was the only institution of its kind in the history of Minnesota. The opening of the State School in 1886 gave a tremendous boost to Owatonna's economic market. Later, as this institution grew, it became an integral part of the community. As the children grew, they provided many families in the area and throughout the state with extra hands through indenture or adoption. Those children who stayed here for an extended time became an integral part of the Owatonna High School--excelling in athletics, drama, and music and in the classroom.

Thousands of children called this institution home for a period of their childhood.

The majority of the buildings on these grounds speak for themselves. They stand strong and formidable. Many have survived the test of time and stand today as a monument of endurance. The city of Owatonna, along with the state of Minnesota, can point with pride to the history and beauty of these grounds and buildings. Nobody can argue with that.

But why was this institution built? What was the reason? What was the motivation?

The ultimate goal--the dollars, the time and sweat poured into this institution--was to provide a home for children who, beyond their control, had the misfortune of a family breakdown. They came from near and far. From farms, villages and cities, from every nook and cranny throughout the state. They came in all colors and creeds and sizes. From birth to 18 years, they came melting together to form the community of the Owatonna State Public School.

Those thousands of children were delivered into the jaws of a strange world known as institutional life. Swallowed up by the necessity to adapt to the culture of the school, each sought a comfort zone of their own. Consequently, each and every child has a different story to tell. But together this is where we lived shoulder to shoulder. Together we worked and played, laughed, cried, ate and slept. We fought and made up. Together we had the measles, the mumps and chicken pox. We had our tonsils removed. This is where we received our early education. We had bloody noses, passed love notes, and listened to the mournful cry of the mourning dove and the lonesome whistle of the freight train. This was our home.

The ancient spiritual teachings of the Cheyenne Indians tell us that we meet ourselves in almost everything we confront. For example, a group of men spending a night on a mountaintop will each have a different experience. One person may be overcome with a sense of awe. Another may spend every moment gripped by fear. Another may sleep the night away. While the mountain is the same, each has brought himself to it, and has a different experience.

So it was for each child who entered this institution. And once you were admitted to the State School, you could take the child out of the school, but you could never ever take the State School out of the child.

How did the school measure up as a home? Without question, it provided the necessities. Unfortunately it didn't fulfill the deepest principles in human nature, the craving to be loved and appreciated. Home is the most important factor of any child's life. Home is the cradle of the human race. It is here the human character is formed--either for good or evil.

But we're not here today to judge the pros and cons of this institution. Rather, we're here today to honor these grounds and most important, to honor the children of this institution. This memorial we are about to unveil was built for this sole purpose so present and future generations will always know that this was the State Public School, the childhood home of thousands of needy children from 1886 to 1945.

May the unveiling of this monument preserve the rich history of this institution for the Owatonna community and the state of Minnesota.

For all of us State Schoolers, may this monument and this day serve for some as a healing of the past.

For others, as a grateful thank you, and for all of us, a reminder of a unique childhood that brought us together as lifelong friends and hopefully made us stronger and better able to survive life's battles.

May the heavens smile on us again today, and may all people here rejoice in being part of this historic occasion. God Bless this place, and God Bless America.

Miracles Continue to Happen

From this humble beginning that was motivated by the desire to remember the children and preserve the history of the State School, miracles have continued to happen. To make the Children's Cemetery more accessible for the public, the city of Owatonna added a new cement sidewalk, and the Orphanage Museum Board began selling boards for a memorial boardwalk. The boardwalk now exists on the former cinder path that brought the children to their final rest during the orphanage era. Today the Children's Cemetery has become a place for prayer, meditation and appreciation. No longer forgotten, the children are remembered almost daily by visitors.

We opened the Minnesota State Public School Orphanage Museum in the corridors of the old Main Building, and it's the only orphanage museum in the nation. The history of the school, warts and all, is shown through photographs, artifacts, stories, audio stations and signage. Creating this museum awakened and propelled the community as Maxine and I put our time and energy into establishing and organizing it. We serve as museum curators, and I speak to individuals and groups who come to look and learn. We talk to about fifty groups each year. We have supervised the outside historical signage and a memorial for Wards who died in World War II, and a recreation of the original rock garden.

In 1995, a family in Waseca found a silent film, shot in the 1930s, that shows children of the State School engaged in various activities, I added a narration, and today we show this film as part of our museum tour and talk. Although the children in the film are idealized, and nothing remotely negative is shown, one gets a good impression of the population density on those 300+ acres, and of the energy generated by five hundred children who lived within the campus.

In 2002 Maxine and I were instrumental in helping produce an award-winning documentary, *The Children Remember: Life at the State Public School for Dependent and Neglected Children.* Thirteen former State Schoolers reminisce about their experiences, and excerpts of the historic '30s film are featured in the documentary, along with highlights of my successful campaign to revive interest in the school and erect a memorial. The film earned a premiere showing at the Minnesota History Center and a Certificate of Commendation from the American Association for State and Local History.

Another project completed was re-facing the root cellar. Built in 1886 and expanded in 1922, this structure is an historic reminder of how the institution stored summer vegetables and fruits for feeding its population throughout the cold of winter. Flowers on the ground, a State School tradition, now grace the lawns during summer, and the grounds are immaculately groomed by the City of Owatonna.

We mail out a quarterly newsletter to nearly a thousand people who either grew up at the school or have expressed an interest in being kept updated about the progress of the museum, and we maintain a website at www.orphanagemuseum.com. All work is performed by volunteers and funded by donations and grants. In 2002 the Minnesota Historical Society held its Annual Preservation Conference on the grounds, now called West Hills, to showcase the preservation of the State School site.

Today the city of Owatonna takes great pride in the State School preservation, and there are plans to restore one former cottage, Cottage 11, where my brother and I lived for many years. This will give tourists a good insight to how the children lived in a cottage. Approximately five thousand people visit the museum and walk the grounds each year, and a commonly heard comment is, "I learned something today."

In 2006 the Preservation Alliance of Minnesota selected the Minnesota Public School Orphanage Museum as one of Minnesota's 25 best-preserved historic properties. Maxine is convinced that the Lord had a plan and purpose for our lives, even before we were born. He put both of us through a lifetime of experiences and gave each of us special talents to help share the State School story.

Maxine's leadership, clerical and organizational skills were a great asset. I had the knowledge, background and charisma to tell the story with humor and compassion. Finally, the Lord gave us the support of so many great people. The blessing is that the door that opened in 1952 bringing Maxine and me together for a lifetime has ultimately touched so many lives.

Maxine has been a tower of strength throughout my adult life. She has stood by me even though I have given her plenty of reasons to leave. I honestly believe the reason she has put up with some of my behavior is that she came from such a good, solid family, rooted in faith and family.

I can't find the words to express my appreciation and love for her understanding, compassion, patience and love. Without her I'm like half of a pair of scissors. She has been a wonderful partner through life, and for that I will be eternally grateful. My children, Rob and Cheri, have always been so special to me too. If I have given them half the happiness they've given me, then my life has been a success.

Getting to Know my Siblings

Over the years after leaving the State School, I eventually met all my siblings. However, each had gone on to live a life totally different from the one I lived, and we didn't have much in common. Even if you are a blood relative, if you're separated as children and then see each other occasionally for a few hours, it's very difficult to pick up the pieces. Of course, when we did get together we talked about how interesting it would have been if we had grown up together. But that was just not meant to be.

Since Oscar and I spent many years at the State School together, we knew each other as brothers. Consequently we've kept in very close contact, and we know and understand each other. We have always maintained a close relationship. As Oscar stated a few years ago in a letter, "We have shared many memories, and we were never alone as long as we had each other."

Hazel, my oldest sibling, has always been the glue of the family. She lived with the family that took her from the courthouse that day until she was an adult, and she made a genuine effort to honor our mother's wish that we stay together by staying in contact with Oscar and me through letters that kept us informed of where all our other siblings were. Other than Oscar, Hazel has been the closest to me throughout the years, our substitute mother. I owe Hazel a special thank you for helping me meet the rest of the family. I doubt I would have ever known them without her help, and I will always hold a special place in my heart for Hazel.

Leonard, my oldest brother who was eight years older than I, served in World War II and made his home in northern Minnesota. He was very reserved, and we only saw each other a few times.

Ruben stayed in the Morris, Minnesota area and farmed the majority of his life. He was a hard worker with a quick wit. I would stop and visit him occasionally, and we always had a good time. He liked to razz about our dad, Eddie, and recall his antics.

I never knew Hallen, because she died before I was born. Verna married a farmer from Madison, Minnesota and was a lifelong homemaker. She was three years older than I, and it took time to get to know her. It seemed there was a barrier, but in her later years, we developed a very warm relationship.

Ruth, who was two years older than I, married and moved out of Minnesota, so I never got to know her very well. Whenever we'd meet over the years, it was always at a family occasion so we've never been able to develop a close relationship.

Gladyce, my only younger sibling, is most like me. Although we didn't see each other at all during our childhood, and we don't see each other very often now, we are very close and keep in contact by telephone. Leonard, Ruben and Verna have passed away. It's a shame circumstances prevented me from growing up with this family. For the most part, my own children didn't get to experience knowing their aunts, uncles and cousins on my side. There will always be that void in their lives.

On July 3, 1993, Maxine and I presided at the dedication ceremony for the State School Kids Memorial, Cemetery and Museum.

169

Although there were once hundreds of orphanages in the United States, our orphanage museum is the only museum of its kind in the country.

Oscar, Gladyce and I at a recent get-together

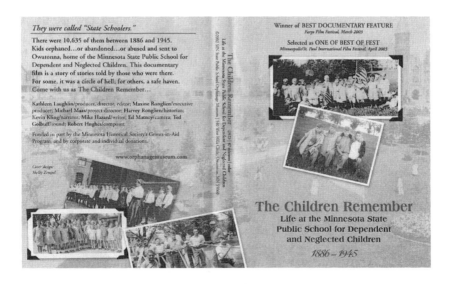

Our documentary video, "The Children Remember: Life at the Minnesota State Public School for Dependent and Neglected Children," was selected as one of the Best of Fest at the Minneapolis/St. Paul International Film Festival in 2003.

A little girl pauses to remember Lloyd Reed, a child buried in the State School Cemetery.

To the children who rest here, May the love you lacked in life now be your reward in heaven. You are remembered.

The State School Cemetery
"We Children Remember; We Will Not Forget"

I've shared a great deal about the children who lived through the State School experience, but it's important to remember the 198 children buried in the State School cemetery. This became their final resting place when they were unclaimed by their families.

In their honor, I share the following tribute, which I felt privileged to present in August, 2004, when Owatonna celebrated West Hills History Week as part of the town's sesquicentennial celebration. Approximately 250 people attended this ceremony, many of whom were State Schoolers who returned for a special reunion weekend.

"As part of this reunion day, it is only appropriate that we spend one half hour at this cemetery to remember and pay respect to children who rest here.

"On behalf of every State School child, deceased or living, from the bottom of my heart I thank everyone here this morning who cared enough to come and attend this service. Thank you all for remembering the 198 children buried on this hallowed ground. And when I say thank you, I speak with a thousand voices for the thousands of children who were placed in the State School Orphanage. These 198 children died too young. Maxine and I have calculated from the records that the average age at death was 4 years old. So young and innocent, they surely couldn't have left a blemish on this earth.

"To give you a stark contrast to the way news is handled today, the headline of an obituary in a 1902 newspaper reads, 'Grim Reaper Claims Another State School Child.'

"Without family, most of these children were buried quietly with little ceremony. There were few, if any, to weep at their graves--or leave a flower of remembrance. Some were buried under cover of darkness because they died of a contagious disease. Maybe this was done to prevent panic within the orphanage population and the Owatonna community.

"We don't know why, but at some point the state stopped putting up tombstones. Thus, 151 of these children were buried here simply identified by their case numbers etched on a cement slab. These children were not only deprived of a family in life, they were also deprived of their very names in death. And sadly, for decades these children, almost without exception, were buried, forgotten, and their graves seldom visited.

"The good news is that one man in our community cared and acted. His name is Bud Blekeberg, and he is here with us today. In 1992 Bud came to me and said, 'All these children should not be forgotten. I'd like to build a memorial.' Next came Bud's idea to erect crosses inscribed with each child's name--151 of them.

Bud accomplished that goal. "And so today, in 2004, we have joy--joy that as a community we have unlocked the cemetery gate. The graves can be visited, and the children remembered.

"Folks, in my heart I like to think this is what happened. I believe that God in his infinite mercy and goodness, looked down from heaven at this orphanage, and when he wanted another little angel, he entered our nursery or hospital and knelt by the bedside of the sick or injured child. Then he put the small hand of the child into his own powerful and gentle hand and softly whispered, 'I've searched throughout the land, and because you are so special, today I have chosen you. Come with me. I have a place for you where love abounds. I want you to come live with me in one of my mansions.' And so it was that he took 198 of these precious children to be with him.

"A few years ago, the folks at Lutheran Brotherhood were motivated to erect a Guardian Angel in one corner to watch over these forever children night and day.

"As sure as we're gathered here this morning on this hallowed ground, and as I speak, I'm confident that these children are looking down and reassuring us, 'I'm content. I'm fulfilled. I'm loved because now I'm in God's kingdom.'

"The State Public School existed for sixty years, during which 10,635 children were placed there. Now, fifty-nine years after its closing, this day could very well be its finest hour. These children are remembered. "

A few months later, in 2005, Linda (Logan) Will, a State Schooler wrote: "I was so impressed by the meaningful ceremony at the cemetery during the reunion in 2004 that I wrote this poem about it."

Children's Cemetery
by Linda (Logan) Will

Gently falls the winter snow
To clad small markers in each row
Rows and rows of stones with crosses
Clothed in lichen, leaves and mosses

Recall the day we gathered there
To honor with speeches, hymns and prayer
"The angels" Minnesota's innocents
No longer abandoned, neglected, dependent

Rustling leaves of maroon and gold
Touch boardwalk and headstones that number his fold
Cottages leveled, fields gone, and yet
We children remember; we will not forget.

My Views on Institutionalizing Children

If you had been in the State Orphanage for as long as I was, there's a good chance you would have come out like I did, physically strong and healthy. Institutional life will do that by providing three healthful meals a day, regular exercise, no snacks between meals or at bedtime, and a regular routine that includes getting up every morning at 6 and going to bed every night at 7:30. If you had been a child who followed this regimen, you would most certainly have developed a healthy body.

On the other side of the coin, without any love or individual attention from adults, you would be emotionally and socially crippled.

The Effects of Institutionalizing the Child:

While this may sound contradictory, I loved the State School. The environment was clean, the beds were warm, we knew the routine, we had three meals a day, a good education, and we learned a good work ethic. During the Great Depression, we State Schoolers may have been more comfortable and well fed than many children who were living with their families. I made many lifelong friends and had many happy experiences there. It was my home, and it tore me up to leave.

What more could I have asked for as a child? Well, over the years I've learned, often in a hard way, that growing up in a large institution leaves many lifelong scars. This has been further verified as my wife and I have visited with many other former State Schoolers and their spouses. Many of us suffered

177

serious inadequacies in knowing how to build a healthy home, a family, and a relationship.

What went wrong? By the natural order of things, we belong in a family unit. This is true even in the animal kingdom. We were conceived by a man and woman, who in a perfect world would love, guide, and protect us. In other words, we weren't born to be raised in an institution. It goes against the grain. But it's an unfair world, and things happen. Yet, that doesn't make a system like the one we had in Owatonna the best solution to a difficult problem. We all crave love and appreciation, and people don't receive either in a large institution.

I'd like to compare putting children in a large institution to putting animals in the zoo. You can feed them, protect them, and bed them down. They are healthy specimens, aren't they? But then, after a few years of captivity, eighty percent of them fail to survive in a natural environment because they didn't learn the skills they need to survive outside the zoo.

The way new children were treated at the State School provides a prime example of a child not being given the chance to learn basic emotional coping skills. A child who has just received the deepest wound his psyche will ever absorb, has been abandoned by his or her mother and father, for whatever reason. Sent to the orphanage, a large, strange place, the child does the natural thing. He or she cries. Immediately the child is slapped and told, "We don't cry here." The lesson taught time after time in a large institution is that you aren't allowed to show your emotions or feel your feelings. There isn't time for such foolishness. The child will cry silently in bed until sleep comes.

You don't have to be an intellectual giant to realize this unnatural stifling of emotions and feelings will forever affect the character of that child.

In large institutions, life is very similar to life in a prison. In fact, in early newspaper articles, children in orphanages were called "inmates." Life in any type of institution is rigid and loveless. Although you are clothed, fed, educated and housed, your emotional needs are starved. The skills you learn to survive and find a comfort zone are much different in an institution than in a family setting.

Psychologist Alfred Adler, an authority on child behavior in the '30s, made this remark. "Even in a model orphanage, the children live like inmates. Emotional starvation is inseparable from institutional life." He warned, "There is danger ahead."

John Steinbeck in *East of Eden* says, "The greatest terror a child can have is that he is not loved, and rejection is the hell he fears--and with rejection comes anger, and with anger some kind of crime in revenge for the rejection, and with the crime, guilt. And therein is the story of mankind."

If you can recall a story I wrote previously in the chapter about our matrons, eleven children I know about from Cottage-11 had either turned to crime, suicide, alcohol or experienced mental problems. One would have to assume that many of the others faced challenges as well. Some problems may have been the result of nature, or inherited illnesses or natural disposition, but most stemmed from lack of nurture. Let me give you some examples.

I've often wondered how much the State School did affect us. I believe you have to take into consideration the age at which the child entered institutional life, how long he was there, the cottages he was in and the matrons who ran those cottages. Was the child's character formed before he entered the school, or was his character formed at the school? I've often wondered why so many of my childhood friends went in such different ways. Here's a glimpse of a few of their lives.

After World War II, my brother Oscar had been discharged from the military and was hanging around Owatonna, not sure of his future. Art, a State School friend and discharged soldier, came through town. He and Oscar went out, had a few drinks, and talked of their military experiences. Art asked Oscar if he had saved any money while in the military. Oscar related that he had saved a few thousand or so. Art asked where he put it, and Oscar replied, "The First National Bank." Not long after that, Oscar went to the bank to draw out some savings and discovered that his account had zero balance. He was shocked! He explained to the bank officials that he had never made a withdrawal. To make a long story short, Art had gone into the bank the very next day after their conversation and relieved Oscar of his money.

Here's how it happened. While in the military, both Oscar and I sent money orders to Jule Keefe, our former matron, who would deposit the money in our savings accounts. Consequently, no one at the bank knew what either of us looked like. So Art goes into the bank as Oscar. The teller questions Art because his handwriting doesn't compare to that on our money orders. Art's answer is that he was wounded in the war and had to learn to write all over again. After much discussion, the teller gave in, and Art walked out of the bank with Oscar's savings.

Eventually Art was tracked down, convicted and sent to jail. This was only the beginning of Art's lifelong history of crime. Today, in 2006, Art is in High Desert State Prison in Susanville, California, serving life without parole for murder. He shares his cell with one other "cellie." Art is a triple bypass survivor who is 80 years old, in a wheelchair and deaf.

I am his only outside contact. He writes often, reminiscing about his early childhood and days at the State School. Needless to say, he has plenty of time. Oscar carries no animosity. Instead he says Art was a different kind of guy who couldn't overcome the twists and turns of his childhood.

I correspond regularly with Bob, another State School friend who now lives in California. Bob lived an institutional life because he came to the State School as a young child and remained there until he was a teenager. He lacked the drive to make it on his own, a perfect example of a person brought up in a welfare state.

Life has been difficult for Bob. His brother Bill was killed in World War II, and Bob received his life insurance settlement. After that ran out, Bob turned to the government for assistance. Unable to hold a job, he has no family and lives a meager existence. I have always had a spot in my heart for him. His letters always start out, "To my best friend in the whole world." A few dollars I send now and then for a little extra spending money brings great joy to an "old SPS buddy," as he signs his letters.

Another interesting story is the life and death of Frederick Berndt. Frederick spent his entire childhood at the State School. Information given us by his friend, Yolanda Thompson, tells a story of a brilliant, very talented man, yet he couldn't handle his personal life.

He became a college professor, yet ended up on the streets of San Francisco penniless. His marriage failed, and he lost track of his two children. Near death at age 80, he was being cared for in a hospice. He begged the staff to call me. Although he had never returned to the State School, his dying wish was to be buried with his State School friends in the Children's Cemetery. After going through many hoops and hurdles, I informed the hospice worker we would honor Frederick's wish. Within one week Frederick died. His ashes were shipped to me, and with the help and cooperation of many in our community, we gave Frederick Berndt a Christian burial, laid down a bouquet of flowers, and erected a cross that bears his name. May he rest in peace.

Another State Schooler, Don, ran the gamut of state institutions that included the State School, Red Wing Reformatory, St. Cloud Prison, and finally Stillwater State Prison. While an inmate at Stillwater, he was taken to the University of Minnesota Hospital for treatment. After escaping from the hospital, he was shot down in front of the Goodwill store in St. Paul. A few days before he was shot, he told my brother Oscar that they would never take him back alive. He couldn't take being cooped up any longer.

I want to inject, however, that we had many success stories too. Many State School boys went into the military and served honorably. Those returning home from World War II took advantage of the GI Bill to receive college educations and home mortgages. One of my best friends became a school superintendent. Another became the director of a YMCA. Many became farmers, accountants, teachers and coaches. One became a meteorologist, one drew a nationally syndicated cartoon strip called "Maggie and Jiggs," and many ran their own businesses. Many went on to be good parents and providers, and two from my era wrote award-winning books about their lives. They may have had to tackle problems caused by their upbringing, but they succeeded in spite of those problems.

When you warehouse children for a long period of time in an institution, they become institutionalized. The children I grew up with were told when, how and where to do everything. You learn not to question authority. Just do what you are told. Authorities do all the thinking for the child, which causes the child's creativity to become dull. The dull child lacks the skills to accept responsibility and to develop a will to get ahead. The child becomes so accustomed to being taken care of that when he or she becomes an adult, he still needs someone else to lead him.

This is comparable to what happens with longtime prisoners. When they are released, they often commit a crime to get sent back to prison because they need the walls of an institution in order to survive. They can't make it on their own. This happened to a lot of State School kids.

Another problem evolved from orphanage life. Whenever a child is brought up without positive adult interaction and role modeling, the child has little knowledge of how to build a successful life and family. Unless this adult child gets help, he or she will more than likely fail at the very thing he wants most, maintaining a healthy home and family. It is no wonder the divorce rate is so high among State Schoolers.

I look back on my own life. Since I spent almost my entire childhood in an institution, I knew nothing about family. When Maxine and I met, I didn't know what cousins, uncles, aunts or in-laws were. I didn't know you celebrated birthdays.

When we got married I couldn't get it into my head that I was now part of a family. Many times I wouldn't go to family functions. I'd say, "I didn't marry them. I married you!" If Maxine would talk me into going, I'd sit and sulk and ruin the day for everybody. I never had a conversation with an adult as a child, only "kid talk" with my peers. I feared that I couldn't make small talk. A lady recently told me, "Now I understand the behavior of my father-in-law, who was raised in an orphanage. Whenever company would come, he'd get up and go out in the field." I could relate.

Being brought up by women, I had no male role models. What did I know about being a spouse or a parent? Absolutely nothing. Family is invaluable. If you are fortunate enough to be raised in a good, loving family, it's easy to take them for granted because they are there for you the first thing in the morning and the last thing at night, day after day. Like our good health, we take our family for granted and fail to appreciate it until we lose it.

From the perspective I have gained today, I think that I failed at the very thing I wanted most, to be a good parent. I short-changed my family without realizing it at the time, but I learned a lot after I knew it all. My trust level is very low, and other State Schoolers have also spoken about their lack of trust. For example, if I have a letter to mail, I don't trust that another person I give it to will mail it. I have to mail it myself. I have always blamed the institution for my lack of trust because there was hypocrisy and a discrepancy between what we were punished for and what we saw some of the people in charge getting away with doing. We probably weren't too smart, but we weren't dumb either.

When I went to Hazelden for alcohol treatment, my counselors forced me to delve deeper into my past. My psychologist explained that my sense of trust was no doubt shattered before I ever went to the State School. When I lost my mother, and then my father, I felt abandoned. Then, when I was not chosen as my brothers and sisters left from the courthouse, and when I was not even allowed to stay with my brother Oscar, I felt abandoned again. When I was shuffled around between three homes before I was taken to the State School, I became even more detached from care-giving adults and kids my own age. I had to find a new comfort zone with each new shift, and the only person who was consistently present in that whole tumultuous upheaval from one situation to the next was myself. My final move to a large institution came when I was only 5 years old, and by that time I had learned to not count on much. Even though I don't remember these events, I lived them and they are buried in my psyche.

Another factor that affected my trust level was that people were constantly moving in and out of our lives, often with little or no warning. We all learned to be cautious about developing a bond with a best friend. As likely as not, that friend would one day disappear with no explanation except that somebody took him. It was very rare to ever hear from someone who had left. I think sometimes school authorities confiscated the letters because they didn't want us to be enticed to run away to a place described by someone who had moved on to greener pastures.

I still have a penny postcard sent to me on January 7, 1943, by my pal Harold Betin. He addresses me fondly as "Goonhead," and says he's having a "swell time" in St. Paul, despite being hospitalized for a hernia operation. He sends regards to some of the other guys and asks me to tell them to drop him a line. He signs off with, "Your best pal, Harold." I hung on to this card through the years because it was rare. In most cases, when your best pal left, you would never hear from him again so you simply sucked it up and went on.

After World War II, I was told Harold died of spinal meningitis he contracted during basic training. Fifty years later, in 1994, I had a chance meeting with Owatonna resident Myron Sandberg. Myron told me he was in the service with a State School kid named Harold Betin. Did I possibly know him? I told him that Harold was my best friend, but that I had heard he died of meningitis. Myron said that he had actually died after a boxing accident. I was stunned to learn that Myron knew Harold, and stunned to find out how my friend had died. A small world!

I've also come to realize that I missed learning about many aspects of daily life by not living with a family. When I became an adult, I knew nothing about money, bills, writing checks, insurance, buying a car or home, borrowing money, celebrating normal family events like weddings and anniversaries, and the value of education. It sounds strange, but I didn't even know how to gauge what to wear and what activities to plan by taking into consideration the outside temperature. We State Schoolers were never exposed to discussions about everyday matters that go on within a normal family. When adults talk about various topics at the dinner table, on a Sunday morning after church, or while riding in the car, children absorb and ask questions about what's going on. Even when the parents think they aren't paying attention, little ears listen. A kid who has never heard any conversations between adults has a huge void in his understanding of the world when he enters the adult world.

We were raised with a herd mentality. Everything we did, we did en masse. When we went somewhere we lined up two by two, shortest to tallest, and a cottage full of boys went to the dining hall or the church together. Adults seldom gave us any individual attention, and if they did, it was usually in a negative way. The best way to avoid negative attention was to blend in. The matron didn't have time for one-on-one conversation.

Humans deeply crave love and appreciation. Every child is deserving of dignity and is worthy of love. I don't care if you were born in a mansion or a shack, if you were raised in a loving family, you're going to have half your life's battle won by the time you leave home. If you weren't loved and appreciated, you'll need help along the way to build a successful life.

I once read about a convicted murderer who was asked if he had any last words before being led to the gas chamber. He answered, "I'd rather be wanted for murder than not wanted at all."

Home is the cradle of the human race. It is where our character is fashioned, either for good or evil. Some children have the bad fortune to be orphaned, neglected and abused. Our social system is still struggling to figure out the best way to help these children. Currently they place them in foster homes, because children obviously can't take care of themselves. Some older children go from one unsatisfactory foster home to another or back and forth between a foster home and their less-than perfect natural family. They often develop antisocial behavior and an inability to bond. The child welfare system is far from perfect.

In 1910, Congress established widows' pensions, which allowed a mother to provide for her children when the breadwinner of the family died. Part of Franklin Roosevelt's New Deal was the establishment of a program to provide aid for dependent children. These government assistance programs allowed otherwise destitute women to keep and raise their children, and this, along with other social welfare programs, reduced our need for orphanages.

There are now subsidized guardianships that allow relatives to raise orphaned children. By the end of the 1950s, orphanages were virtually extinct in the United States. Children didn't need to go to institutions any more.

I've been asked many times recently for my opinion of the proposed return to orphanages. For the past dozen years or so, debate has been raging about whether or not we should build new orphanages to accommodate certain children.

I have many questions about this proposal. Who would be served? How would it work? How would staff be trained to work in such a place? How would modern laws protect children and staff against abuse and allegations of abuse? This is a complex issue involving money, politics and child welfare, and it's difficult to make a definitive statement.

Orphanages vary. By 1930, 1300 orphanages existed in the United States, and it's no coincidence that the number hit its peak during the Great Depression. The orphanage in Owatonna was the third largest in the nation. Over the years there were twenty-two smaller orphanages in Minnesota, most of which served their local areas or communities. Most were run and financially supported by churches, religious orders, or other philanthropic organizations.

Many children placed in orphanages were not actually orphans by the strict definition of the word; some still had both parents, and others were half-orphans whose one living parent could not take care of them properly for one reason or another. Children admitted to privately operated orphanages would not need to permanently sever ties or guardianship rights with their natural families so they often returned to their families within one to four years, or when circumstances allowed it. Since we State Schoolers severed legal family ties by becoming Wards of the State, we did not have that option.

In a twelve-year study of a half million institutionalized American children, University of Chicago researchers confirmed that very few institutionalized children are ever adopted. My personal experience could have told them that. Children either aged out, were placed out on foster care situations or indenture contracts, or they ran away. Most never experienced life in a family until they married and had children. Only five percent of State Schoolers were adopted.

A system like the one we had at the Minnesota State Public School for Dependent and Neglected Children would be impossible in our country today. Modern laws prohibit adults who are not family from forcing children to do heavy work like we did at the State School on the farm, in the laundry and on the grounds, and they do not permit indenture contracts. Child abuse laws would help convict people like Miss Morgan, along with any adults who witnessed her actions and who, by their silence, became accomplices to her crimes.

Today's orphanage would need to be an entirely different place. It could not be self-sufficient like the State School was because the logistics and liabilities would be a nightmare. Today's orphanage would have to be open to scrutiny from the outside world, and it would have to be prepared to take care of children until they reached adulthood.

I cannot relate to group home orphanages that house only 10-16 children, nor to Boys Town, which doesn't accept children until age 12 and then keeps them only two years. Children at Boys Town live in small family units with parental role models. I can only relate to the type of experience I lived through.

Maybe small group home orphanages with parental role models are effective if enormous amounts of money are available to build and maintain them with a caring, educated staff. Otherwise, I'll stand by my statement etched in granite on our State School memorial plaque in the West Hills complex. "In my opinion, the legacy of the Minnesota State Public School for Dependent and Neglected Children is that the environment generated in a large institution is not conducive to raising emotionally healthy children. Let the museum, cemetery, and outside memorial forever serve as a reminder of that truth, and as a remembrance for every child who passed through these doors and their struggle to overcome the scars left by this institution."

A Boy From C-11

Staying in Touch

Because I stayed in Owatonna, I've had the opportunity to visit with hundreds of State Schoolers who have returned to town and looked me up over the years. Many have phoned me. I've had phone calls from all over the United States, from California to Maine. One night a State Schooler awakened me with a phone call from Australia. We have a strong bond, and I never tire of hearing about their adventures.

It's interesting to hear their stories, and it gives me an interesting insight to human behavior when I note that everybody looks at their experiences in different lights. Everybody has his or her own opinion, and that's the way it should be because even though we lived in an institution that tried, for the sake of simplicity, to create a common experience for all us kids, we are all different, and we all processed that experience differently.

I have heard stories in which the same kids were in the same cottage at the same time with the same matron. One will say he never saw a matron hit a child, and the other will say kids were getting beaten regularly. I don't argue with any of them. That's life. Sometimes I believe we have selective memories. Eye witnesses don't make good witnesses. Ten people can see the same crime committed, and each reports a different recollection, even under oath in a court of law.

One evening during the 1960s, when we lived on South Grove, a man came to our door. My son Rob answered it and came to let me know there was a weird man asking for me. I went to the door and there stood a man in an oriental outfit with a big smile on his face. It was Carroll Tomar, and we began talking a mile a minute. Rob went to his mother and asked, "Who's that guy anyway?" She told him it was another of Dad's old State School friends, and that seemed to be all the explanation Rob needed.

Carroll Tomar came to the State School as a baby and was with me in C-11. Carroll was always into something as a kid, and it quickly became evident he hadn't changed as an adult. He led me to his car, and it was filled with cameras. I asked where he got them, and he laughed and said, "Don't worry about it. Do you want a few real cheap?"

I learned a short time later from my brother Oscar that Carroll Tomar was killed a few days later. Someone broke into his Minneapolis apartment and shot him dead before he could get out of bed.

Ev Lindorff, another of my C-11 friends, stopped in and captivated our family with his war experiences. His ship was sunk in the Battle of the Coral Sea. He related how he and a buddy were standing by the bulkhead and the ship was sinking fast. Ev said to his buddy, "We better get moving." His buddy just stood there so Ev grabbed him by the arm and the buddy fell flat forward—his legs sheared off above the knees. Ev floated on a piece of wood for many hours before being rescued.

A few years ago, while I was entertaining some students from Dodge Center, a young boy piped up, "Did any of you ever amount to anything?"

I replied, "Your school superintendent is a State Schooler. His boxing trunks are hanging in the museum!" His mouth dropped open. True, Marv Tenhoff, another of my State School buddies, graduated from St. Olaf College, became a teacher, continued his education and later became a superintendent.

My best friend the entire time I was at the State School was Ev Lindoff's brother Curly. Curly became a millionaire overnight when he won the Arizona Lottery. He sent me a newspaper clipping that showed him being presented with the winning check. He included a little note asking how everything was with me and adding, "Just wanted you to know that your old C-11 buddy is a millionaire." Then in large print he advised me in no uncertain terms NOT TO GIVE HIS ADDRESS to any State Schoolers.

I thought, "Good for Curly." Then I decided to write him a letter. In the first couple of paragraphs I bragged him up about what a great guy he was. Then I said, "Curly, don't you remember that nice summer afternoon, right on the corner of the C-11 playground, when we made that blood vow that if either of us would ever come into a fortune we would gladly and willingly (and I underlined those words) share it with the other guy?" Then in parentheses I reminded him that I was the other guy.

I didn't know mail could travel so fast. It seemed like almost the next day I got a letter back. CURLY DIDN'T REMEMBER! So I wrote a letter back to him and told him I didn't remember either. Curly was in town last summer, and darn, I still haven't gotten into that billfold of his. That's life in the fast lane, I guess.

Often I'll get a phone call from a child or grandchild of a former State Schooler. Their loved one has passed away, and they have questions about what his or her childhood was like at the State School Orphanage. They were either afraid or they neglected to ask questions when they had the opportunity.

Sometimes I can help them on the phone, and other times they ask if I can personally walk the grounds with them to explain life at the orphanage. Sometimes they'll tell me that the information I give them helps them understand certain behaviors, habits, likes and dislikes that became a permanent part of the former State Schooler's life.

They'll say things like, "So *that's* why she always got up before dawn and went to bed so early," or "Now I know why he insisted we always clean our plates at every meal." How rewarding it is to meet these people who were also affected, although indirectly, by life at the State School and explain about our daily routine and about how and where we lived and played.

Occasionally I will even have lived in the same cottage with the individual. To watch their faces as I relate certain incidents that I shared with their loved one is a rare treat. One particular day I had three sisters who came to learn about their father's life at the school Sure enough, he was one of my old buddies, and we found his picture in the museum.

To share laughs and tears of years gone by with these family members who are hungry for information makes all the work we do worthwhile. The hugs of sincere appreciation I receive from them create memories I will cherish forever.

As I've evolved from Ward of the State, to school alumnus to museum curator, tour guide, reunion organizer and historian, I've had some State Schoolers tell me I glorify the State School. Others say I'm too hard on the school. That's okay. Sometimes I honestly believe I was born to be a State School kid. There were many...I was but one. It was my destiny to become a conduit between the past and the present. I didn't make history; I recorded it. And after more than seventy years' connection to the Minnesota State Public School for Dependent and Neglected Children, I am glad I was able to do so.

A 1938 photo of all the kids and staff.

Epilogue

Thank you for taking the time to read my story. My hope is that you have not only found this book informative and interesting, but that it has also given you some new insight into the history of the era when the Minnesota State Public School for Dependent and Neglected Children was running strong. Memory is unreliable; it disguises and distorts. I've heard that all memoirs are attempts at inventing the truth. They test the writer's integrity and demand constant striving for fairness and truth. Fairness and truth have been my ultimate goal when writing this memoir.

The State School Orphanage Museum

540 West Hills Circle
Owatonna, Minnesota 55060

Hours are 8-5 Monday through Friday.
Enter through the Main Building doors.
Weekend hours are 1-5.
Weekend visitors enter through the blue doors
of the Owatonna Art Center,
located at the rear of the Main Building.
More State School Information can be found on our website:
www.orphanagemuseum.com.

To order additional copies of this book for your library,
historical society, school, church, or to give as a gift,
send $13.95
plus $3 shipping and handling to:

A Boy From C-11
P.O. Box 925
Owatonna, MN 55060

Make checks payable to "A Boy From C-11"
Minnesota Residents add 90 cents Minnesota Sales Tax